PUPILS WITH PROBLEMS
rational fears... radical solutions?

PUPILS WITH PROBLEMS
rational fears... radical solutions?

Philip Garner

Trentham Books

First published in 1999 by Trentham Books Limited

Trentham Books Limited
Westview House
734 London Road
Oakhill
Stoke on Trent
Staffordshire
England ST4 5NP

British Cataloguing in Publication Data
A catalogue record for this book is available from the British Library
ISBN 1 85856 134 5
(hb ISBN 1 85856 133 7)

Designed and typeset by Trentham Print Design Ltd., Chester and printed in Great Britain by Alden Press Limited, Oxford.

CONTENTS

Introduction

'Human history becomes more and more a race between education and catastrophe' (H.G. Wells)

Like a lot of things in life, this book set out to be something else. In its early days it was intended as a considered, realistic and measured analysis of what was happening to those who have, since 1994, been termed 'pupils with problems'. The original outline proposal, containing the usual suspects when it comes to chapter headings in books on this subject, went through several changes in direction and overall focus. In truth, though, there was a niggling thought in the back of my mind that I was still replicating material on the subject that already exists, some of which is of particular relevance and potency. I didn't want to reinvent any wheels. So, during this period of planning and reflection I found myself recalling the honesty of many of the 'problem' adolescents that I had worked with some ten years or so ago. Whilst not excusing their sometimes merciless intent on the ritual crucifixion of teachers, social workers, some of their peers and others, they had (and still possess) a capacity to 'tell it like it is'. It occurred to me, at this point in the gestation of the book, that I was being far less forthright than the pupils who were to be the subject of my gaze.

The initial idea thus metamorphosed into something quite different. And perhaps there are grounds for considering it to be a more honest interpretation of the topic, for a number of reasons. 'Pupils with problems' is a wide-ranging and emotive term. It is a complex and frequently controversial aspect of educational practice. Whatever else it is it is certainly always regarded as newsworthy, as recent media exposure concerning the inclusion of apparently disruptive pupils testifies. Much of what goes on in this area of work, perhaps more so than in many other aspects of education, is highly individualistic, frequently informed by under-lying cultural values and prejudices, and undertaken in the full glare of a public which has been fed a routine diet of tales of dis-ciplinary collapse in our schools, chaos and vandalism. Typical of the emotive journalism which feeds the myth is a caption in a recent article in *The Independent* (Thursday, 9 July, 1998), which was entitled 'Riot Acts'. The piece, which was used as part of a two-page spread bemoaning the 'fact' that 'schools are having to cope with a rising tide of yobbishness', identified six pupil-distur-bances between March 1995 and June 1997 to illustrate the gravity of the trend. Whilst not underestimating the problems which may exist in a small minority of schools, it doesn't take a genius to ascertain that six disturbances in 28 months in 28,000 schools in England and Wales, hardly constitutes a crisis.

Notwithstanding the public criticism of schools and teachers that invariably follows such media exaggeration, that same public nevertheless expects 'solutions' to a feature of contemporary schooling which is as old as formal education itself. Nor can it be said that such solutions are readily available: indeed, the applica-tion of particular approaches, prescribed by both official sources and theorists as 'cures' (such as the current unquestioning allegiance to assertive discipline by an entire Local Education Authority's schools, or by the largely fanciful preoccupation with bootcamp-type punishment for even very young delinquents) is a potent example of the reduction of human beings (pupils) to the inanimate and unthinking. This book, correspondingly, is neither an academic tome based wholly on collected data, an apologia, a scholarly treatise, nor a polemic. What it has become is a mixture of opinion and measured argument, supported by data and recollection from nearly thirty years in mainstream and special education and, latterly, in higher education.

The use of the term 'solution' in the title of this book, therefore, must be seen in part as an ironic observation on the quest by suc-cessive governments for help based on piecemeal and disjointed policies. These have ultimately served only to sustain the status quo: they continue to deny the rights of pupils, are blind to their individualistic cultures and they fail to deal with those structural factors which have long been regarded as both endemic within our society and major contributory factors to the process of disengagement experienced by large groups of young people. Such solutions are more likely to be directed towards local interventions, as in the case of Circular 1/98, which required Local Education Authorities (LEA) to provide 'behaviour support plans' (although given the systematic asset-stripping of the LEA's financial capability to deal with the issue this smacks of a blame the victim approach). Some of the small-scale approaches and the principles that inform them, are the basis of this book.

Each chapter is built around, either in whole or in part, what pupils with problems (a term which itself is indicative of a particularised way of thinking about children – as I will discuss) and the teachers who work with them, have to say about their respective situations. This is evidence from the front line, with all of its sensationalism and the prospect of the charge of a failure to secure an appropriate level of intellectual rigour. To those who would argue that the use of anecdotes, hearsay and the kinds of qualitative data that many in the research community refer to in derisory terms as being 'soft', and therefore easily 'disproven', I would offer a an alternative validation.

For generations it has been the case that the voice of the child, the pupil or the student, and those who advocate on their behalf, has been pigeon-holed as a device that could be used for the vicarious advancement of official policy, based entirely on rhetoric. It has been a common characteristic of recent reports and policy documents that some tacit, but ultimately meaningless, acknowledgement has to be given to the viewpoints of a population who have education 'done to them'. Similarly, too, there has been a carefully politicised use of teachers' views, best illustrated by the official adoption of the 'teacher as researcher' mode at a time when educational research is being systematically denigrated as distant from the reality of the classroom. This book makes use of both sets of informants in its attempt to arrive at an informal agenda of considered action.

'Pupils with Problems' is the term coined in 1994 by the government of the day to describe those children and young people who were perceived, by nature of their oppositional behaviour, to present a challenge to the established order (DfE, 1994a). The term has subsequently become an accepted category or grouping. Its very adoption cocked a snook at all those who have struggled to implement the Warnock commitment to an end to labelling. So who exactly decided that it is the *pupils* who have the problems? There is a perversity about a belief-system subscribed to by faceless individuals whose moral code allows free trade in arms, a blind-eye to, or even a casual acceptance of, the systematic violation of human rights, and the ever-widening gulf between rich and poor – and yet who have the brass neck to target and then condemn those individuals who have always been isolated, on the margins and 'at risk'. It beggars belief, as we are about to enter a new century, that we continue to be suckered into thinking that the next under-funded educational action zone will make things all right when it is patently clear that we need to look further than schools to find the solutions. Indeed, the widespread adoption of the term 'pupils with problems' is an indication of a need for a fundamental change in approach to young people. The size of this task, and its implications for existing hierarchies and procedures, means that it falls far beyond solely educational initiatives – but this has largely been rhetorically accepted or denied, according to political affiliation, from time immemorial.

The reason that the construction of this book significantly changed direction at such an early stage was to allow exploration of some of the themes which I feel are at the heart of this vast area of concern and which are of overriding concern to those centrally involved. But I resolved to do this on the basis of what I felt strongly about, supported by the commentaries, protestations and critiques of pupils and their teachers. Like many of the pupils and teachers that I have encountered in recent years, I find it impossible to subscribe to a hypocrisy which embraces inclusivity in education and social care yet makes it explicit that only those who conform to a prescribed set of regulations and protocols will benefit. In one highly personal sense, therefore, it represents a cleansing of the soul. But from another perspective its intention is to present alternatives to the tired re-workings and aimless policy directives which have studiously missed the point of the story. The young people who are the subject of this book represent the descendants of those generations by whose efforts the eventual rewards of stockbroker, banker, spin-doctoring political ad-man and post-modern wheeler-dealer were set in motion. In previous generations they were products of the forge of labour-supply, who were encouraged to seek employment at a level which ensured their compliance with the codes of the day. Now, with the massive post-1960s shifts in work patterns, their services of sinew and muscle are no longer marketable. Financiers, industrialists and politicians have largely taken the rewards and run, and are still doing so. All that remains is the waste-product of their self-interest and a guilt assuaged by the financial pittance thrown the way of the disaffected, disenfranchised and jobless.

Ultimately, too, I have become tired of the race to rationalise, in terms which many might regard as essential to claim academic respectability and empirically justifiable, the differential treatment of young people by the education system of England and Wales. There seems to be little soul left in that endeavour. I recall sitting in on one of my first teachers' in-service sessions after moving into higher education; I was treated to an exquisite rebuttal of the need to justify a phenomenon solely in terms of the weight of quantitative, empirical evidence. An experienced tutor challenged the importance which we give to the size of a sample in providing 'proof' of a given educational phenomenon. He emphasised a traditional, folk-psychology explanation: the spoken word, as data, is both reliable and valid in terms of the speaker as an individual actor, and should be recognised and valued as such by the recipient. For the special educator this was a master-class, demonstrating the impeccable credentials of case-study or child-focused study in research. Following his example, I can say that in this book the data I use is unmeasured, from a quantitative point of view. My own addition to the theory so cleverly articulated by my erstwhile colleague is that you can't put a price on passion or feeling; the impact of just one young person's problematic behaviour cannot be reduced to an inanimate numbers' game. It is a real action, affecting real people and should be dealt with as such. In consequence the words and pictures I draw upon, whether of the pupils, teachers or others involved with them, should be considered as free-standing, coherent and incontrovertible messages in their own right.

The use of the term 'pupils with problems', as I've said, has been problematic from the outset. It suggests that, if these young people really wanted to, they could deal with their own problems. After all, such forbearance in the face of adversity served us well in the Dardanelles and Dunkirk, didn't it? I do not intend to provide an exhaustive essay on the arguments for or against the use of the term 'pupils with problems'. My own view is that the expression suffers from many of the drawbacks of an equally ambiguous and indefinite term – emotional and behavioural difficulties (EBD). Or those inherent in the use of such deficit-laden and stereotyping expressions as 'disruptive pupil', 'disaffected pupil' or, in fact, the 'naughty' child. All are terms whose range and complexity of interpretations and meanings is matched only by the number of people providing them.

In recognition of that point of view which suggests that behaviours are behaviours in context (Hargreaves, Hestor and Mellor, 1975), and that, axiomatically, definitions are best constructed within the same context, I have retained the use of the term 'pupils with problems' because of its official status in the present educational context. Nonetheless, there are occasions when, for the sake of meaning, continuity or to make an explicit point, 1 substitute another term from the lexicon that now applies to pupils whose behaviour is perceived to be inappropriate and falling short of that which is expected by teachers and schools.

In summary, then, this book does not provide an incremental treatment of pupils with problems, nor is it a manual on good practice. What it seeks to provide is a critique of some of the concerns that surface whenever discussions on pupils with problems arise. In parts it offers reflection on these; elsewhere it provides anecdote. But throughout I have tried to make use of the viewpoints of the two groups most crucially involved: the pupils with problems themselves, and their teachers.

Though the book's content, interpretation and subsequent commentaries are my own responsibility, there are, nevertheless, a number of people who have provided support, inspiration and professional insight. Although the content of the book may fall short of the passionate illumination that many of these individuals have brought to my personal and professional life, to allow their influence to go unacknowledged would be wrong. It is also true to say that my work has always been celebrated by my family, and I owe them much gratitude for their forbearance. In particular I would like to thank Ann for her support and for continuing to provide a haven of peace, because....

Most of my work in teacher education has coincided with a period of extreme scrutiny of the education service generally, and of teachers in particular; it has also run parallel to the activities of successive governments whose interpretation of social justice is has been characterised by a 'you're first after me' mentality. But negative inspiration is a fine thing. I'd like to thank successive governments for the way in which they have continued to ignore the voice of children who behave in ways deemed inappropriate; for the way in which the specious rhetoric of official guidance has masked a withering, defeatist and barren approach to education in general and to that of these children in particular; for the way in which thousands of good teachers have been sacrificed in the name of 'reforms' which, as J.K. Galbraith has noted, do the word itself a disservice; and for the manner in which these governments have continued to allow protocols and bureaucracy to dictate the ethos of schools, classrooms and individual relationships. I'd also like to acknowledge a population which has, for the educational equivalent of tax-cuts, a new microwave or two-weeks in Fuerteventura, allowed such governments to proceed with the kinds of educational legislation which would give totalitarianism a bad name and whose style of consultation makes Machiavelli's grasp of power-sharing seem liberal. Where were you (us!), for example, when LEA support services were systematically being ravaged by legislation? More apposite to this book, where are those in authority or privilege who are going to fight tooth and nail for the cause of pupils with problems? After the conferences of teacher-unions in the Spring of 1998 it appears that they are unlikely to be found amidst the battalions of the rank-and-file: a far cry indeed from thirty years ago. So, no miners under the hooves of horses here, no streets filled with protest. And a final 'thank-you' for the self-seeking mannerisms it seems we have all too easily learnt from a lengthy period of unenlightened despotism. It is perhaps fortunate that such desperate and forlorn visions can serve equally to inspire and maybe sustain an anticipation that our futures cannot ever be darker.

Chapter 1

Where do they come from and where are they going?

'The past never lies providing you read it dispassionately,' Jim Bowen always used to tell us in our A-level History class. This advice is a good point from which to begin. The 'careers, routes and prospects' of pupils with problems appears to have hardly changed at all from the 1960s. If anything policy and practice have become more unforgiving and punitive, indicating our inability to read dispassionately the lessons of past failures.

Parents, teachers and those politicians with particular ideological axes to grind have always been concerned about poor behaviour by children and adolescents, both in and out of school. I recollect animated discussion on the subject in my childhood, with the adults around me regretting the declining moral standards of the time. Likewise, one of the preoccupations of social scientists and others during the last ten to fifteen years has been to trace the historical parallels of right-wing social policy in England and Wales (Pearson, 1983; Nelken, 1989). Law and order and education have been the twin fetishes of successive Tory governments during the period 1979 to 1997, the consistent subject of right-wing rhetoric, planning and action (Pitts, 1988; Dale, 1979). The two overlapped, became symbiotic and, for mainstream Tory activists and their supporters in the 1980s, assumed the proportion of a Hydra, in respect of adolescents. In response to what was reported in the press as 'the avalanche of lawlessness threatening to engulf our civilisation', the then Chief Constable of Manchester called for 'labour camps' for 'young thugs'. The focus of the outpourings from both men was that group of young people, usually male and often black, who inhabited certain parts of major conurbations in England and Wales. These were adolescents who were characterised as threatening a '...rising tide of anarchy and violence' (Jenkin, *op.cit.*). This is a tale which has been told with some regularity during the course of the last hundred years, and bears closer scrutiny because it strongly suggests that we haven't yet got the message. This has been clearly spelled out by both the repeated failure of official policy-initiatives and the anecdotal responses of any number of those working with 'pupils with problems': that punitive, rule-governed and non-inclusionary practices will evoke only an increase in the scale and intensity of pupil resistance. The merry-go-round shows little signs of slowing, now that the early mists of promise have become fogged by New Labour's desire to demonstrate a seamless inheritance of New Right initiatives – summarily exemplified by the announcement of 'jails' for 14-16 year-old delinquents (*The Guardian*, 15 April, 1998).

All our yesterdays... some of our tomorrows?

A stereotypical image has been constructed by right-wing activists for both individuals and groups falling into that categorisation so colourfully described by the Chief Constable; this characterisation has even been echoed in some of the critical enquiry into why this should be the case. These young people were seen as oppositional to school and underachieving within it (Willis, 1977), likely to engage in delinquent behaviour (Emler and Reicher, 1995), and from largely working-class backgrounds, often with significant disadvantaging conditions (Mortimore *et.al.*, 1984). The parallels with the 19th century are all too apparent. Over 150 years ago, Fletcher's statistical studies identified four themes which can be viewed as correlates of present-day problem behaviour by juveniles: criminal activity, illiteracy, gender and the spatial location of these activities within towns and cities (Fletcher, 1847). Fletcher linked 'moral' and 'educational' statistics in his studies, an association which reveals much about Victorian attitudes to educational under-performance as well as the durability of this way of thinking right to the end of the twentieth century.

Similar stereotyping has also been evident in the polarisation of beliefs concerning the actual cause of such behaviour and the nature of subsequent intervention. Those representative of the so-called 'tough on crime' element, much in evidence in the Tory party throughout the last twenty years, held criminal activity 'to be solely the individual's responsibility – economic and social causes are dismissed or downplayed' (Hutton, 1997) so that there is

> ...an increasingly shrill cry to remoralise society – in which morality is regarded as the prohibition of individual actions backed by repressive legislation. Economic and social reforms, which might address the causes of these problems, are seen as a return to what has failed; instead, moral individuals, smacked at home, caned at school, wary of steep punishment in prison fixed by automatic sentencing, and who keep their families together are our only hope against future social implosion (Hutton, *op.cit.*, p.17).

Conversely, the brutal stereotypification of social workers, care-workers and teachers working with 'problem pupils' resembled character assassination (Lewis, 1977), and so-called progressive, child-centred policy-makers were similarly derided (Walker, 1977). Sheldon (1994), for example, regards 'Social work, like aviation, as a scandal driven industry', often surrounded by controversy and threats of punitive reorganisation by central government – itself an action steeped in historical precedent, as illustrated by the fearful exhortation of Cabot: 'Let us criticise and reform ourselves before a less gentle and appreciative body takes us by the shoulders and pushes us into the street' (Cabot, 1931).

The historical pedigree of the deficit-laden view of both (delin-quent) juveniles and those who work with them has been as legi-timated now, as it was historically, by the use of a scientific rationale, which justifies the notion of an 'underclass' in two ways. In one version the wealthy simply 'deserve' their success because they have worked hard to maximise their potential; theirs is prosperity which has not been won at the expense of the (urban) poor, who, in any case, are not 'morally' equipped to succeed (Murray, 1990). This is a view which finds its terminological ancestor in the 'moral defective' of the late 19th and early 20th centuries, who presented '...great difficulty. Prison does him no good, and he may be too... wicked for an institution for ordinary defectives... he must be under firm discipline, with plenty of occupation' (Potts, 1917). The educational parallels in respect of pupils with problems are obvious.

The historical impact of this ideological orientation has been well-documented in England and Wales (Humphries, 1981; Pearson, 1983). In 1669, for instance, a protest by children led to a petition to Parliament, in which they described their suffering in

> A Modest Remonstrance
> of that intolerable grievance
> our Youth lie under, in the
> accustomed Severities of the
> School-discipline of this Nation
> Humbly presented to the Consi
> deration of the Parliament
> Licensed, Novemb. 10. 1669.

Subsequently, in the nineteenth century the twin effects of urbanisation and industrialisation resulted in a perception that the traditional societal structure, based upon the tenets of deference, duty and paternalism, was being eroded. In its place a new order was being created, in which a new industrial work force was being characterised as disorderly, potentially criminal and impervious to the hierarchical control exercised with gusto in preceding generations (Wirth, 1938; Levine and Campbell, 1973). Indeed, Lebas (1981) describes the historical and political role of the city as '...significant in that it constitutes... a sense of place from which to organise and resist'.

Again there is a sharp distinction between the belief-systems of the protagonists in this debate, as evidenced in two contrasting extracts from news of that time:

> Under the influence of our humanity-mongers, we have nursed and fostered a race of hardened villains... well the public is now learning, in rather a startling fashion, what is the natural

result of making pets of thieves and garrotters. (*Manchester Guardian*, 2 November, 1862)

Money should be spent on the real punishment of criminals, instead of squandering the hard earnings of honest mechanics and working men and making them objects of interest to idle spinsters and gaol chaplains of the maudlin class'. (*The Observer*, 30 November, 1862)

The 'cycle of disadvantage' (Rutter and Madge, 1977; Townsend, 1979) and the debilitating effects of poverty on educational achievement (Mortimore and Blackstone, 1982; Kumar, 1994) have been a consistent part of the machinery of social and economic renewal in England and Wales throughout the last 200 years. With a 'new' central government anxious to make its mark as enlightened and reformist there has been a call to address underachievement, failure and a commensurate decline in levels of acceptable behaviour in school. Typically such calls for intervention have focused mainly upon disadvantaged urban populations, who have predominantly been at the epicentre of 'problem' behaviour, and who, but for the sanitising veneer of political correctness, would still publicly be termed an (educational) underclass. That the dominant political attitude being sustained currently in England and Wales appears, on the face of it, to be rather closer to the Victorian (aka. Thatcherite) idiom should continue to be a matter of considerable concern.

There has long been a middle-class recognition that certain parts of towns and cities constituted a considerable problem. Ashworth (1954), referring to the 1840s, remarked that '...Overcrowding and congestion, poverty and crime, ill health and heavy mortality were shown to be conditions commonly found together...'. Here it was that *Gemeinschaftlich* relationships had supposedly been driven asunder by the impact of the *Gesellschaft*, in which '...the household become(s) sterile, narrow, empty, and debased to fit the mere conception of a mere living place... (it is) nothing but shelter for those on a journey through the world' (Tonnies, 1955). This was, and still is, the heartland of oppositional behaviour – an observation which would be hideous in its determinism if it did not need to be reconstituted to act as probably the single most obvious indicator of the unjust allocation of educational capital.

A typification of this urban 'struggle' has been the consistent and conspicuous failure, throughout the last 200 years, of the education service, often working closely alongside social services and charities, to meet the needs of significant numbers of children and young people in these metropolitan locations. This shortcoming has been noticeable in two aspects of education: academic achievement and social behaviour. It is the latter which comprises the focus of this chapter. It has formed a focus of attention in recent history. Pearson (*op.cit.*), for example, indicated that, in 1977, one government minister offered

> ...a flexi-time history according to which, in the same speech where he entertained the spectacular belief that Britain's streets had been plunged into insecurity 'for the first time in a century and a half', he also conjured with a more modest time scale whereby 'such words as good and evil, such stress on self-discipline and standards have been out of favour since the war (p.8).

In the schools themselves this situation was articulated both by academic failure and a perception that standards of behaviour were declining. Although even the former assertion is debatable, the latter has been shown to be largely a matter of fiction (Elton, 1989). Both views were widely promoted and popularised by right-wing academics and politicians, and publicised gratuitously in a series of forbiddingly titled 'Black Papers' (Cox and Boyson, 1977).

The depressing and deficit-laden picture of contemporary adolescent life in urban areas is simply a re-presentation of the educational and social landscape obtaining in England and Wales in the mid- to late 19th century and the early part of the 20th. A number of common themes can be found which are as important now as they were then. Amongst these are correlations between problem behaviour in school and criminal activity outside of it, illiteracy or low levels of educational performance, the socio-economic status of disaffected school pupils and delinquents, the high proportion of young males involved in such activities, and the segregated spatial location of both the dwellings of the perpetrators and of the schools in which they were educated. These factors were mapped during the middle part of the 19th century by Fletcher (*op.cit.*, 1848; 1849; 1850), and reviewed by Maxim (1989). When compared with more recent statistics the figures show little deviation and illustrate the remarkable incapacity of educational, social or penal initiatives to alleviate the problem (Home Office, 1995). Maxim (*op.cit.*) makes the connection explicit, stating that

> ...it is interesting to note that many of the relationships we currently observe between social-structural factors and crime today were just as significant in the nineteenth century. Indeed, if these results are compared with data from contemporary Britain, the similarities are striking (p.46).

The educational context of oppositional behaviour by schoolchildren at a national level during the early part of the 20th century, described as a series of 'protests by pupils' by Adams (*op.cit.*) has been well documented; a high point was reached in 1911. This coincided with a period of considerable industrial unrest, leading to strikes and other civil disturbances. It was certainly the case that a mood of confrontation had been caught by pupils, such that *The Times* reported that in one location children were 'parading the district and calling upon other schools, asking the scholars to come out in sympathy. Window panes and street lamps along the line of march were smashed and the 'loyal scholars' were beaten with sticks' (*The Times*, 9 September, 1911). What may be significant, given the sharp division between rich and poor which was being increasingly confirmed by the impact of industrialisation and urbanisation, is that of the 68 school strikes recorded by Adams (*op.cit.*) as taking place between 1911-1917, all but five took place in towns or cities which replicated the 'degradation of urban life' characterised, for example, by the writing of Mayhew (1861), Engels (1892) and Booth (1896). They were also predominantly in the North of England, subsequently to be a frequent location of industrial strife, poverty and educational and social unrest, representative of a more recent phenomenon summarised by Byrne, Williamson and Fletcher (1975) as

> ...towns so often described as the depressed industrial areas of Britain, the industrialisation and depression seemingly inseparable. Many northern towns, whose industrial legacy has often meant large-scale unemployment, figure predominantly... The poor material environment of these areas is evidenced by high population and household densities and the poverty of social amenities in the community (p.71).

One of the locations of school disturbance at that time was Manchester, on which the next section of this chapter focuses.

Education and delinquency: learning how to blame

The 1916 conference of the National Special Schools Union was notable for a comprehensive account of juvenile crime provided in a paper by Spurley Hey, then the Director of Education for Manchester. At that time Manchester Education Committee, which had the responsibility for the education of about 130,000 children (under 14 years), was sufficiently concerned about the '...undeniable evidence of an increase in juvenile offences' (Hey, 1917) to conduct an inquiry into the extent and nature of the phenomenon. The broad statistics show that, from the period January 1911 to December 1915 inclusive, 2741 cases were considered by the Juvenile Court. Over 92% of these were committed by boys, with a chronologically incremental increase in tendency to commit offences between ages 7-12 years. Of these '...many... are dull children, varying in mental capacity from slight sub-normality to actual mental deficiency' (p.20). By far the most significant spatial concentration of offending behaviour was the administrative ward of Hulme (Medlock and St. George's). Relatively few offences occurred in wards such as Withington, Didsbury, Crumpsall, Blackley or Openshaw. The phenomenon was thus dramatically concentrated in 'problem' areas of the city – locations which, moreover, and in spite of the impact of gentrification, remain largely disadvantaged today.

Hey provided a substantial commentary, in which he identifies eleven factors explaining the extent and nature of juvenile crime in Manchester. One relates directly to education, while the remainder have been subsequently confirmed as important negative factors on the educational progress of adolescents. Fletcher's (*op.cit.*) four causal factors, identified several generations previously, predominate in the explanations given by Hey.

1. Illiteracy

Hey's perception was that many of young people committing offences also performed poorly in school. These, he suggested, would require the most educational input in order to 'eradicate or minimise crime'. On the other hand, and as Hey confirms, '...teachers and officials agree that the leaders of juvenile gangs are alert and precocious – boys of super-normal rather than of sub-normal intelligence'.

A further link with education is provided by Hey's belief that, as a result of the introduction of compulsory education, there was a significant difference in educational attainment between parents and children, to the detriment of the former. As Hey comments,

> Children have discovered that they could correct their parents in speech; could solve a sum in a shorter time and by a better method; could air their French at home without danger of correction; could inform their parents of facts of earth, sea, and sky; and they attach more importance to fact-knowledge than to the knowledge that springs from experience (p.19).

This perverse twist is illustrated by the example of a child of 9 who refused to obey her father because 'he can't do my homework'.

The most substantive reference to educational factors as a cause of problem behaviour are outlined under a section entitled 'School Rearrangements', within which Hey identified three strands. The first related to school-buildings: the onset of the Great War resulted in 30 schools in Manchester being transferred to the military authorities for use as hospitals. Wholesale disruption of schooling ensued, partly as many children failed to attend the Education Committee's 'special outdoor work' arrangements. There was also a significant absence of male teachers, again as a result of the Great War; this was viewed as highly problematic, given the prevailing belief that '...although some women are better disciplinarians, even with boys, than some men, it must be conceded that, generally speaking, masculine government is best for boys' (p.27). This is linked elsewhere to the absence of male social workers, notably those who organised recreational activities after school or during the school vacations. In their absence, as Hey is given to comment,

> Boys are thrown more on their own resources. Many have withdrawn from the influence of the clubs, and it is a fair assumption to make that some at least who have done so have misdirected the qualities of initiative, courage and endurance which the clubs have striven to inculcate (p.30).

Finally, the shortening of the school day – partly in the interest of economy – meant that children had more opportunity to misbehave. This threw

> ...many of the children accustomed to street-playing into the street for a longer period, because, in the case of working mothers, very frequently the house is locked up when the children return from school. There is an increased possibility of mischief under the circumstances (p.27).

As a further reminder of the historical continuities of the problem, and the degree to which academic underachievement was inexorably linked in peoples' minds with delinquency, Carson (1936) made what is now a pejorative generalisation that 'There is (then), in my opinion, a very close relationship between mental defect and juvenile delinquency. I firmly believe that between 50 and 60 per cent of juvenile delinquents are of defective intelligence' (p.41).

2. Socio-economic position

There is a significant correlation, according to Fletcher's data, between problematic behaviour and economic disadvantage. He goes on to describe what, for many, has become the stereotypical version of the Victorian city. Thus, in the industrial districts, the workers lived near the mills, factories and workshops in which they were employed; these '...do not make for pleasant or healthy surroundings... there are no allotments, and few and small open spaces; housing is dear, families often large, and overcrowding is common' (p.30). As a direct response to this, Fletcher believed, the inhabitants of such areas look 'for a change' which, he rather pejoratively states, they find in the '...comparatively roomy, attractive and almost palatial music-halls and picture-houses' (p.30). Parents' attendance at such places, he argues, is a major reason for indiscipline amongst their children: such places of entertainment were chiefly concentrated in those wards of Manchester which showed high indices of disadvantage.

3. Gender

Hey's data provides ample support for the widely held belief that it is boys, rather than girls, who engage in delinquent activity – and also form the bulk of pupils causing problems in schools. Again there is a powerful contemporary parallel to be drawn. From 1911-1915 the number of offending girls in the City of Manchester fell from about 13% to just over 6% of all offences committed; meanwhile the proportion of male offenders rose steadily, commensurate with the decrease shown by the girls. Over 72% of cases of juvenile crime in the period were related to theft or 'breaking and entering'.

Some of Hey's descriptions of individual cases, whilst in hindsight appearing somewhat comical, nevertheless lend qualitative support to the statistics he presents. He reports, for instance, on the large proportion of offences committed by 'boys who organise themselves for criminal purposes'. He provides examples of this kind of behaviour as amplification for this observation:

Six or seven boys. Gang known as 'The Black Hand'. Met under arch of Central Station every evening. A fire was lit and plunder divided.

Four boys. Known to each other as 'Dick Turpin', 'Galloping Dick', 'Buffalo Bill' and 'Hard Riding Dick'. Convicted of breaking in and stealing (p.13).

In contrast, girls are rarely mentioned in the qualitative data: Hey's most frequent reference is in respect of so-called 'brothel cases' where, for example, a 'Girl used by mother to invite men to enter house'. Girls were seldom the perpetrators of breaking-in to households or vandalism.

4. Spatial location

The cartographical representation of the incidence of 'problem behaviour' provided by Hey is all that one would expect, given the disadvantaging conditions obtaining in certain parts of the city. His description of the lack of facilities in the central area is bleak. The density of population in the central zone is over three times greater than that of the northern or southern fringe areas. One indicator of the sharp discrepancy in the levels of amenity is the discrepancy in the amount of 'open spaces'. The two outlying areas have 44 amounting to a total area of 1384 acres but the central area has only 25, totalling a mere 96 acres – and it is here that most problematic behaviour is recorded. Subsequent assessment of the 'image' of each of the wards used by Hey in his data presentation suggests that little has changed.

Modern Times: the motorcycle of disadvantage

Since the time of Hey's small-scale research in Manchester each of the causal factors underpinning both problematic performance in school and delinquency have continued to form part of a vicious self-fulfilment rooted in disadvantage and prejudice which is a major characteristic of certain urban locations. Rutter and Madge (*op.cit.*), Mortimore and Blackstone (*op.cit.*) and Kumar (*op.cit.*) have all confirmed the link between disadvantage, educational under-performance and problematic behaviour, while Plaskow (1985) observes that the whole period marked

> ...the triumph of the thought police ... not conscience, which made cowards of (nearly) all of us, out of fear and self-pre-servation. Yet there was a dramatic paradox in the mismatch between rhetoric and the pressures towards normative, compliant behaviour. Power was promised to the people in the name of democratic pluralism. The reality was of punished deviance. (p.199)

Malik (1993) has provided further powerful indictment of the final years of Thatcherite hegemony in England and Wales, as marked by policies whose negative and deficit-orientated view of adolescents who misbehaved verged on the malevolent. Examining a sample of young people who had been referred to specialist agencies (probation, psychiatric, social services or education) on account of their 'difficult behaviour', Malik's survey did much to recall the pattern which obtained almost 80 years earlier. Those referred, particularly for specialist educational and probation intervention, '...are almost exclusively young men', whilst those referred to social work increase significantly in number after the age of 13. Both groups are largely drawn from single-parent or carer families, where '...only a small number of families of young people admitted to institutions had one or both parents in paid employment' (p.41). Moreover, the disadvantaging context referred to earlier by both Fletcher and Hey in what was an era of social, educational and economic imbalance seems to be in the process of being reinforced, so that

> Professionals within the systems perceived inadequate housing, low income and unemployment as contributing to the families' difficulties, causing worry, anxiety, and depression and having a negative effect on a parent's capability to offer good parenting (p.41).

Of similar relevance is the data provided by the Prison Reform Trust (1991), which reveals some interesting offender-characteristics. Over 40% of all prisoners have no formal education and over half have functional illiteracy. Around one-third of all offenders suffer from some form of psychiatric disorder, at least some of it manifest as 'difficult behaviour'. Over 38% of young offenders have experienced life in local authority care. Although the study does not refer to social-class characteristics, the inference is there to be drawn; it seems inevitable that Galloway's crime map of Sheffield, another city in the north of England, would be replicated, with offenders being largely drawn from the locations showing the highest scores in disadvantage indicators. When viewed alongside the same authors' mapping of school exclusions, which are a virtual replication of the spatial distribution of criminal offences, it is difficult not to put two and two together.

The cant of it all is that whilst this Victorian, even pre-Victorian, distribution of wealth, cultural capital and opportunity (including the opportunity *not* to commit offences) is being sustained, successive governments engage in a the kind of rhetoric that merely confirms the status quo. Attacks by New Labour on single-mothers, educational failure, and 'squeegee merchants' by a combination of 'naming and shaming' and punitive legislation directed (still) towards those least able to cry 'foul', is confirmation that the cycle has become a motorcycle, travelling at speed to ensure that the Thatcher legacy is preserved.

'In the former Soviet Union the past is always unpredictable', so the saying goes. In the case of England and Wales predictability is the watchword for the roots, careers and destinations of a large proportion of 'pupils with problems'. Nevertheless, it is unproductive to dwell on the past in a way which induces collective hand-wringing and a sense of *deja vu*. What happened historically to pupils with problems should only be acknowledged if it can be used as a point of departure for new initiatives and new ways of understanding. In attempting to develop new ways of working, schools and teachers should deal with a collective view of the realities they face. In other words, they need to ensure that policy and practice are hallmarked by the belief that inclusive practice in today's schools should accommodate those pupils who, for as long as we can remember, have been a cause for concern on account of their behaviour.

Chapter 2

Policy and practice in reactionary times (1989-1998)

The Elton Report (1989) contributed significantly to the debate about pupils with problems. It concerned discipline in schools and marked a major initiative by central government to tackle what they saw (or were told by right-wing interest-groups to see) as a growing problem in primary and secondary schools in England and Wales – the difficulties posed by pupils whose behaviour did not conform to the social norms and expectations of schools in general – pupils who had 'problems'. The Report detailed the findings of a *Committee of Enquiry into Discipline in Schools*, and its brief was to 'recommend action to the Government, local authorities, voluntary bodies, governors, headteachers, teachers and parents aimed at securing the orderly atmosphere necessary in schools for effective teaching and learning to take place' (p.11). Mischievously, the Report's summary added that 'We find that most schools are on the whole well ordered', an observation which reinforces the argument that it was more on grounds of 'moral panic' that the Committee was convened rather than on the basis of reputable evidence of a large-scale decline in standards of pupil-behaviour. In all, 171 recommendations were made.

The succeeding decade saw vigorous debate concerning the nature, cause and effects of problematic behaviour by some pupils in schools, the types of provision available, and by various models of intervention. Statutory and guidance documents include the so-called 'Six Pack' of government Circulars, five of which refer directly or indirectly to the behaviour of pupils and its consequences (DfE, 1994a; DfE, 1994b; DfE, 1994c; DfE, 1994d;

DfE, 1994e) and popularised the term 'pupils with problems'. Circular 1/98, relating to the provision which LEAs are required to make for pupils with problems, has also to be considered.

The Elton Report itself, together with the previously established ground-breaking principles contained in the 1981 Education Act, raised a set of important questions for practitioners. In particular, the challenging prospect, subsequently re-defined in the Green Paper *Excellence for All Children: Special Educational Needs* (DfEE, 1997) that all children, irrespective of the nature of their behaviour, should be considered as candidates for inclusion within mainstream educational provision. What I am attempting to do, therefore, is to use the Elton Report as a major reference for the developments which subsequently took place (or didn't) in a field which is 'as old as education itself and is never far from teachers minds' (Varma, 1993) and ultimately concerns the life-chances of those who are located, at best, 'on the margins' of formal, mainstream education (Lloyd-Smith and Davies, 1996).

The recent context

Both the Warnock Report (DES, 1978) and the 1981 Education Act reinforced a view, and an operational reality, that little was then being done to integrate pupils who were regarded as having emotional and/or behavioural difficulties (EBD). The period following the Act showed that, whilst considerable progress had been made towards integrating pupils with moderate, or even severe, learning difficulties into mainstream schools, little was done about the segregated position of children whose learning difficulty was deemed to be associated with problematic behaviour (Swann, 1992). An indication that the education service as a whole was increasingly unwilling or incapable of meeting the complex needs of this part of the SEN population during 1981-1988 is to be found in the continued high levels of exclusions of such children (Blyth and Milner, 1996; Parsons and Howlett, 1996) – still being manifest ten years later (see Chapter 9).

The failure of mainstream education to deal effectively with pupils with problems can be attributed to a number of factors.

The perceptions and professional beliefs of teachers concerning levels of discipline in schools was shown in research conducted by Lowenstein (1975). This indicated that teachers were inclined to believe that incidents of severely aggressive behaviour were commonplace in schools other than their own (Armstrong and Galloway, 1994). It is worth noting that Turkington (1986) argued that the 'disruptive pupil' was an invention of the media utilised by teacher unions to advance their claims for professional recognition and enhancement of salary structures.

Whatever the validity of such claims, it remained apparent that, during the period leading to the Elton Report, teachers in mainstream schools were becoming increasingly militant towards children whose behaviour they viewed as unacceptable. This might be explained by the increasing scrutiny (and frequent negative criticism) of teachers by politicians and others (O'Hear, 1988), causing the Elton Report to observe that '...the status of teachers has declined in recent years' (p.12). Teachers became embattled and because of their own insecurities, fewer were able to empathise with the needs of children who misbehaved in school. A similar situation has prevailed in the decade following the Elton Report, with periodic attacks from politicians, government departments and quangos on teachers, the performance of schools, and teacher education. In consequence, as the present government's own chair of the education and employment select committee has warned, teaching is seen as a 'second-rate profession' (*Times Educational Supplement*, February 20 1998, p.2).

The political climate of the 1980s and the fundamental policy changes of the 1988 Education Act made the Elton Report inevitable. The impact of the Report, and the policy initiatives which were subsequently influenced by it, were greatly compromised by the so-called educational 'reforms' pursuant to the Act. Indeed, when pupils with problems are discussed, it is seldom long before the negative effects of the Act are mentioned – and this book is no exception.

Three elements of the 1988 Act can be implicated in the failure of many schools to implement Elton's recommendations effectively, particularly those relating to the maintenance of 'problem pupils' within the mainstream. Firstly, central government's preoccupation with the establishment of a national curriculum, and the circus of assessment which accompanied it, deflected much teacher attention away from 'social behaviour' as a central issue in learning. Many teachers appear not even to have heard of the Elton Report or be aware of professional development initiatives resulting from funding made available to local education authorities (LEAs) for 'Elton Training'. Given the pace of change and the innovation overload of the period, it is unsurprising that the findings of the Report were largely overlooked.

The 1988 Act also initiated both a devolution of centrally-held LEA resources to individual schools and the introduction of 'open enrolment', whereby parents (and children...) were able to select the school of their choice. These developments combined to herald the arrival of overt competition between schools for both pupils and the funds that accompanied them. In such an environment there are strong indications that many mainstream schools cease to be willing to accommodate behaviours in children which deviated from the norm, for fear of becoming reputed as a 'sink' school (Cooper, 1993). As Armstrong and Galloway (*op.cit.*) put it, 'the very presence of large numbers of children with special needs, particularly where those needs arise from learning and/or behaviour difficulties, may be seen as harmful to a school's performance' (p.186).

To these specific concerns may be added two more general factors. In terms of its demography, the SEN population (and, axiomatically, those who are ascertained to have an EBD, and many others who are regarded as 'pupils with problems') is located in schools in (principally) urban or metropolitan regions with high scores of indicators of disadvantage (Bash, Coulby and Jones, 1985). Such schools, although they frequently have concentrations of pupils with EBD-related SENs, are seldom well-placed to respond to the needs of such students, whether in terms of curriculum provision or support work utilising external agencies. Neither are they attractive to influential middle-class parents whose children may be expected to be high achievers in school. A second, closely related, factor is the high incidence of problematic school-behaviour in children from socially and economically disad-vantaged populations. Further, there is evidence that some groups, notably African-Caribbean children, have been dispropor-tionately represented in recent statistics on exclusions (Parsons and Howlett, *op.cit.*). Each factor implies that a 'cycle of dis-advantage' (Rutter and Madge, 1976) obtains, adding to the com-plexity of the task facing teachers in the post-Elton period.

Painting the arms and legs: a topography of policy and practice

In spite of such negative conditions there is a powerful argument to suggest that the period following the Elton Report has seen both a focused awareness-raising in respect of 'pupils with problems' and a commensurate set of initiatives, at both national and local level, designed to meet their educational needs. The substantive section of this chapter refers to these developments, focusing on a number of key areas, each augmented in succeeding chapters. In attempting this overview, it is perhaps fair to recognise that, just as 'pupils with problems' represent the most contentious of the SEN population, these key issues cannot be viewed as uni-dimensional components, nor are they intended to be exhaustive. Moreover, since there has always been a correlation between problematic behaviour inside and outside the school, as illustrated by, among others, Pyke, Prestage and Dean (1993), Devlin (1995) and the Home Office (1995), easy solutions are unlikely. The development of new initiatives in each of the themes will continue to provide challenges.

(1) Legislation, statutory and non-statutory guidance

Two sets of official documents form the basis of the statutory framework within which pupils with problems and their teachers operate. The first relate to SEN in general: the 1993 Education Act, the Code of Practice on the Identification and Assessment of Special Educational Needs (DfE, 1994b) and the Green Paper *Ex-*

cellence for All Children (DfEE, 1997a). The second refer directly to pupils with problems: the 'Pupils with Problems' Circulars 8/94 (DfE 1994c), 9/94 (DfE 1994d), and 10/94 (DfE, 1994e) and the Draft Guidance on LEA Behaviour Support Plans (DfEE, 1997b). In addition, there are the official frameworks for the inspection of schools (OFSTED, 1995a; OFSTED, 1995b; OFSTED, 1995c), which all placed considerable emphasis on behaviour and its management in assessing the quality of education provided, and the requirements governing the training of teachers, currently Circular 10/98 (DfEE, 1998).

The principles of the Code and the Circulars are enshrined in the former. Inspectors are advised by OFSTED to look for evidence of 'pupils' involvement in the daily routines of the school' and whether the school is presenting 'scope for pupils to take responsibility' and encouraging them 'to articulate their own views and beliefs' (OFSTED, 1995c).

Finally, two international resolutions are significant: the United Nations Convention on the Rights of the Child (1989) and the Salamanca Statement (UNESCO, 1994), both with important directions towards inclusive education.

(2) Initial Teacher Education and Continuing Professional Development

Recommendations 4-7 of the Elton Report argued that the management of behaviour and an awareness of issues associated with it should become a key criterion for the approval of all initial teacher education (ITE) courses. The recommendations for 'in-service training' (henceforth continuing professional development – CPD) were less forthright and specific, although one of six areas for action to improve classroom management skills was identified as 'more specific in-service training' (p.71). Recommendation 9, eschewing such a generalism, stated that 'the management of pupil behaviour should become a national priority for funding under the Local Education Authority Training Grants Scheme from 1990/91 until at least 1994/95' (p.78).

Subsequently the recommendations for ITE contained in the Elton Report have been acknowledged in Circulars 14/93 and 9/92, relating to primary and secondary courses respectively (DfE, 1993; DfE, 1992). The Special Educational Needs Training Consortium (SENTC) has, however, noted an important discrepancy between the two. Whilst 9/92 refers only to 'the ability to *identify* special educational needs', 14/93 asserts the importance of 'the ability to *identify* and *provide* for special educational needs' (SENTC, 1996; p.20, emphasis added). The ability of institutions of higher education (IHEs) to cover in detail aspects of behaviour management has, at the same time, been curtailed by the moves towards school-based training. Recent research on the SEN-experiences of newly qualified teachers suggests that relatively little direct input is being obtained on matters relating to 'pupils with problems' (Garner, 1996).

The Elton Report paid little attention to the role segregated special schools could play in the preparation of new teachers. Few ITE courses are able to include a special school placement, because of constraints of time resulting from the move to school-based training. Nor do they appear to make good use of the wealth of expertise available in such schools, particularly in behaviour management and social skills training, an issue which is further discussed in section 7 of this chapter.

CPD (continuing professional development) for teachers substantially involved with 'pupils with problems' is itself problematic at present, in spite of Elton's exhortations that '...in-service training should be provided through school-based groups. These groups should aim not only to refine classroom management skills, but also to develop patterns of mutual support among colleagues' (p.12). This is, in part, a result of the move towards local financial management systems, in which schools have direct control of their own financial resources, including those for staff development. As little direct input on matters relating to 'pupils with problems' is taking place at Initial Teacher Education (ITE) level, the need for planned and ongoing CPD is essential. Now, however, it is the decision of individual schools to determine CPD priorities, and, as EBD is viewed as a low-status SEN, there may be less willingness to address its constituent issues in a planned series of sessions over a period of time. It could be claimed, however, that EBD has received a substantial proportion of GEST (Grant for Education Support and Training) funding between 1993-1995; furthermore, pupil behaviour and disaffection are priority areas for training provision within the Standards Fund. But cynics might argue that considerably more funds have been allocated over time for training related to 'dyslexia', a category of SEN which carries far more influence (Snowling, 1987).

Similarly, the element of competition for pupils and resources between schools has meant that individual schools can be less willing to collaborate with others in CPD enterprises. This state of affairs is likely to have a deleterious effect on the quality of a teacher's professional development, removing an opportunity to share ideas and good practice with a wide range of colleagues from other schools, backgrounds and areas. More positively, SENTC (*op.cit.*) has recommended that one indicator of common competence for those involved with SEN must be that 'Teachers should demonstrate knowledge, skills and understanding to enable them to devise learning programmes which specifically address pupils' emotional and behavioural needs' (p.34).

Cooper, Smith and Upton (1994) have summarised the post-Elton position. They state that 'Teachers in general are unprepared by their initial training and by in-service training arrangements, for dealing with emotional and behavioural difficulties..., and specialist teachers in the field have been shown to place their requirement for further training in the area high on their list of priorities' (p.3). The observation, by Lloyd-Smith and Davies (1996), that 'Deviant or disaffected pupils have become particularly vulnerable in the education market created in the UK in the past decade', equally apply to their teachers, whose opportunities to learn or refine good practice in both ITE and CPD are now being seriously curtailed. Cole, Visser and Upton (1998) sum it up: 'The patchy and less than satisfactory situation in regard to training painted by HMI (DES, 1989b) would still seem to apply'.

(3) The quest for categories

The period following the publication of the Elton Report has witnessed a continuing debate about the value (and ethics) of categorising of children with behaviour problems. Since 1944 there has been a gradual shift away from categorisation in special education, culminating in its abandonment in the 1981 Education Act. But the controversy continues to simmer, not helped by the vague definitions provided in official (government) documents. Thus, the Code of Practice determines that 'Emotional and behavioural difficulties may become apparent in a wide variety of forms – including withdrawn, depressive or suicidal attitudes; obsessional preoccupation with eating habits; school phobia; substance misuse; disruptive, anti-social and uncooperative behaviour; and frustration, anger and threat of or actual violence' (DfE, 1994b, para 3.64). In similar vein, Circular 9/94 states that 'emotional and behavioural difficulties lie on a continuum between behaviour that challenges teachers but is within normal, albeit unacceptable bounds and that which is indicative of serious mental illness' (DfE, 1994a, p.7).

Definitions regarding pupils with problems need to be clear and precise. But the dangers of self-fulfilment and negative-labelling have long been recognised (Rist, 1970; Rosenthal and Jacobsen, 1968). Some authors have argued that the maintenance of categorisation for problem pupils obscures the real issue. Smith (1990), for example, maintained that 'if the child's needs can be met and problems solved by changing the way in which the school deals with that pupil, then the issue of whether to apply the label of 'maladjustment' or 'emotional and behavioural difficulties' should not arise'.

Cooper (1996) takes the debate a stage further, arguing that it is behaviours rather than individuals that need categorising. He asserts the need to 'recognise the value of a common vocabulary for talking about children's problems'. This recalls the supporting research for the Elton Report, which elicited types of behaviours that teachers encountered or found difficult to deal with. Such an approach might well incorporate the non-judgemental approach characteristic of behavioural approaches successfully.

(4) Models of Intervention

Three principal models of intervention for pupils with problems have been popularised following the Elton Report. The Report itself paid little attention to the distinctions between these approaches, although it did affirm the need for schools to ensure that their 'rules are derived from the principles underlying their behaviour policies' (p.100), implicitly signalling the importance of a corporate management policy which was underpinned by a distinct and shared rationale.

Relatively few schools (usually special schools for statemented EBD children) subscribe to a single model of intervention. Schools generally operate hybrid systems, based on behavioural, therapeutic or ecosystemic approaches. Awareness of the validity of each of these has developed markedly since the Elton Report, as the examples drawn from some teachers' recent written observations (Gains and Garner, 1996) indicate. Some of these are summarised below (see also Chapter 7).

- The Behavioural approach is based upon early theories of learning. Its proponents argue that, as all behaviour (good or bad) is learned, it can be unlearned. Typically this involves learning acceptable responses or unlearning responses which are not acceptable. It is also characterised by an emphasis on behaviours which are measurable (i.e. which can be observed) rather than upon the mental processes (causes) which prompt the behaviour.

- Psychodynamic and therapeutic approaches are based on the view that problem behaviour has its source in the unconscious or subconscious and that even the earliest experiences of infants will affect their subsequent responses to things around them. Psychodynamic theory originated with Freud, who sought to enable patients to review their 'life history' so as to reconstruct meanings for their present behaviour. For the EBD child, the inner world of emotions have remained largely unchanged since early childhood, resulting in a failure to adapt to the outer world.

• The Ecosystemic Approach views all children as belonging to a set of sub-systems. Their behaviour (whether good or bad) is a product of interactions within and between these systems. Bronfenbrenner (1979) was highly influential in applying eco-systems to the study of human behaviour and, in particular, education. He argued that the world of the child comprised a *microsystem* (the child himself), the child and his teacher and classmates (the *mesosystem*), the child and his relationship to school as a whole and to parents and outside agencies (the *exosystem*), and finally the child in relation to the cultural, social and educational values and beliefs of the world in general (the *macrosystem*). Problematic behaviour occurs when there is a dysfunction between these systems.

Each of these orientations is further explored in Chapter 7, in which teachers' views are elicited about their preferred style of intervention. Chapter 7 also provides an important commentary on how the interventions teachers adopt are strongly related to their attribution of causality in respect of problem behaviours and to the terminology they use when describing the pupils.

(5) The Views of Children

The importance of the role of pupils in managing their own behaviour and in shaping and reviewing school policy on behaviour is made explicit in Recommendations 75 and 76 of the Elton Report (p.36). It recalled the earlier work of Rutter *et.al.* (1979) and Mortimore *et.al.* (1988), which evidenced the benefits of pupil involvement in relation to both behaviour and learning. The early 1990s saw growing awareness of the need for such inclusion, as the body of literature shows (see, for example, Galloway and Davie, 1995; Garner and Sandow, 1995), in spite of a prevailing tendency to characterise many pupils with problems as disaffected from learning and even oppositional to schools.

In the year the Elton Report was published, two other events had significant impact on the right of individual children to present their views. The UN Convention on the Rights of the Child (1989) stated unequivocally that 'The child capable of forming their own views shall be assured the right to express those views freely, on all matters affecting him or her' (Article 12). And the Children Act (1989) in England and Wales sought to incorporate the same principle and has evoked a significant shift in working practice for many teachers, particularly those in the residential sector of EBD provision. Regrettably there remains considerable militancy in the teaching profession regarding the efficacy of listening to children's views about their schooling. The General Secretary of the NAS/UWT said on *The News at Ten* (4 September, 1996): 'I reject the notion that children have a right to an education at whatever school they choose' (*paraphrase*). This view was put forward during a news item about a problem pupil in a Nottinghamshire school.

The Code of Practice (1994b) has, nevertheless, recognised the value of incorporating the pupil's view. Section 2.37 recommended that schools consider how they involve children in decision-making about assessment and identification, individual education plans and the process of monitoring and review. Circular 8/94, relating to 'Pupil Behaviour and Discipline' (DfE, 1994b) stated that 'pupils can play a positive role' in behaviour management, and the accompanying Circular relating to EBD (DfE, 1994c) recognised that 'there is a positive association between pupils' involvement and greater motivation and feelings of self worth on their part' and that pupils 'should be encouraged and guided in setting and organising learning goals according to their age and understanding'.

Listening to what (problem) pupils have to say about their experiences can assist schools to become more effective, by identifying those aspects of policy which are not reflected in practical action. This is particularly important for behaviour management, and since 1989 a range of initiatives in primary (eg. Coulby and Coulby, 1995), secondary (eg. Garner, 1993) and special schools (eg. Cooper, 1989) have enabled so-called problem children to play a greater part in the disciplinary organisation of their schools.

(6) Provision

Three forms of provision have prevailed since the Report. Pupils with problems are educated either within the mainstream, in off-site units or in special schools. Each has its own characteristics, and attendant potential and pitfalls. The debate surrounding them essentially relates to the efficacy of inclusion, a central argument for all SEN since the Warnock Report of 1978.

Most pupils with problems continue to be maintained in ordinary (i.e. mainstream) schools. There is little doubt that Elton's focus on this sector of provision proved to be a major factor in this, as this chapter goes on to show. The Report's recommendations for mainstream schools were comprehensive and have been instrumental in many of the changes in orientation, particularly in management style, apparent in the 1990s. Thus, Clark, Dyson, Millward and Skidmore (1995) could report that mainstream schools 'were responding to behaviour management as a whole school policy' and ensuring that 'specific behaviour management initiatives were not viewed in isolation but were set in the context of broader approaches to personal and social education'.

Nonetheless some mainstream schools, because of the post-Elton market orientation of education, are ambivalent about the presence of pupils with problems. There are indications that some schools are internally segregated; withdrawing pupils with problems from certain classes or activities. Some schools have on-site units for so-called disruptive pupils. Such strategies can scarcely be termed 'integration'.

The Elton Report failed to recognise the important contribution that special schools could make in assisting mainstream institutions to develop or refine management strategies for pupils with problems. Although it recommended that 'All LEAs should review the alternative provision that they make for the most difficult pupils' (R.86), it did so mainly in the context of so-called off-site units.

Little contact takes place between mainstream schools and segregated special schools. The notion of 'clustering' has been increasingly proposed in the post-Elton period. This concept had developed during the 1980s so that schools could form 'a relatively stable and long term commitment among a group of schools to share some resources and decision making about an area of school activity' (Lunt, *et.al.*, 1994). But there is reason to think that special schools for EBD children are viewed suspiciously and their contributions disparaged (Rimmer, 1994), and this not helped by their exclusion from ITE and CPD, as noted by Bovair (1993).

In 1989 Her Majesty's Inspectors (HMI) published a survey of provision for pupils with EBD which summarised the findings of HMI resulting from their visits to 76 special schools and units between 1983 and 1988. They were highly critical of current provision. Laslett (1990) describes it as '...a disquieting report, both in its content and its implications. It shows... (that) officers from local authorities, personnel from supporting services, and the staff of schools and units, are not meeting the needs of children with emotional and behavioural difficulties' (p.108). HMI noted that '...there were examples of good practice to confirm that the educational needs of EBD children can in fact be met through good curricular planning, sound organisational arrangements and effective teaching. The evidence indicates that the difficulties in achieving this goal through the provision of small special schools and units are considerable' (HMI, *op.cit.*, p.14).

Given the state of the education 'market', such negative statements might well serve a useful purpose. Special schools for EBD children, particularly residential facilities, are costly to maintain. Since the 1988 Education Act LEAs have had diminishing financial resources for placements, and EBD pupils are effectively competing with other, higher status special needs for available monies. As Rimmer (1990) notes, 'The price tag attached to the most desperately needy of children will be revealing of managerial thinking about provision'.

Off-site units, and the Pupil Referral Units (PRUs) established after 1994, represent a point at the middle of the provision-continuum between mainstream and special schools. A major post-Elton development has been the regularisation of this kind of provision. Prior to 1989 there was considerable evidence of its *ad hoc* nature, particularly in respect of referral procedures (Blyth and Milner, *op.cit.*). Such units had 'distinct advantages over maladjusted schools... in that children can be placed in them without the embarrassing and delaying safeguards of special education procedures and with only minimal consultation with parents' (Bash *et.al.*, *op.cit.*, p.116).

Circular 11/94, coyly entitled 'The Education by LEAs of Children Otherwise than at School' (DfE, 1994d), acknowledged Elton's warnings over the *ad hoc* nature of much off-site provision (p.154) by placing the new PRUs on a firm statutory footing and by providing explicit guidelines concerning referral, curriculum and reintegration. This has led to some improvement in the functioning of such units (Normington and Boorman, 1996, although Her Majesty's Chief Inspector (HMCI), maintains that 'standards of attainment in the pupil referral units inspected thus far are variable, but generally too low' and that 'overall the quality of teaching in the PRUs inspected fell below that found generally in mainstream primary and secondary schools' (HMCI, 1995, p.5). Although it is perhaps too early to assess the efficacy of PRUs, their current situation, as outlined by HMCI, does appear depressingly reminiscent of the off-site units of the pre-Elton period (Garner, 1996).

There is now a requirement, articulated in the Guidance on LEA Behaviour Support Plans (DfEE, 1988), that each lLEA 'prepare and review a statement detailing the arrangements made, or proposed, in their area for the education of children with behavioural difficulties'. There are some indications here of worthy initiatives, although they hardly provide radical or new ideas. With some notable exceptions they comprise top-down recommendations and strategies, with only peripheral mention of the routine involvement of pupils in the planning process. LEAs have borne the brunt of successive governments' policies that have rendered them unable to meet the financial demands of 'the arrangements' requested. At best, therefore, the jury is still out.

(7) Developments in schools

The Elton Report acted as a catalyst for many new school-based initiatives designed to assist teachers manage pupils with problems. The same innovations have, in part at least, been of material assistance in enhancing the educational and social opportunities of the pupils themselves.

The development of whole-school policies on pupil behaviour is not new (see, for example, Saunders, 1979). The Elton Report not only stated that 'Headteachers should create the conditions for establishing the widest possible measure of agreement on these (*behaviour*) standards and how they will be achieved' (p.24), but recommended that both 'Headteachers and teachers should encourage the active participation of pupils in shaping and reviewing the school's behaviour policy in order to foster a sense of collective commitment to it' (R.76). Many schools have now established mechanisms by which both groups can participate in policy for formulation.

(8) Ethical and Philosophical Concerns

Each of the foregoing issues needs to be considered against a background of some important ethical and philosophical considerations for the way in which pupils with problems are educated. Some of these, including pupil-rights, the principle of inclusion and equality of access to curriculum and other resources have already been referred to. There are, however, two further issues which are more exclusive to pupils with problems: the popularity of assertive discipline and the use of drugs in the control of young people.

Assertive discipline (Canter, 1982) is based upon the principle of 'integration through shaming'. An explicit statement of rules and expectations is combined with a tariff of escalating consequences for non-compliance. According to Bush and Hill (1993) this secures the childrens' 'right to learn' and maintains the teacher's 'right to teach'. Application of such a strategy can go as far as 'physical intervention and isolation' (Cooper, Smith and Upton, *op.cit.*) but at the very least involves the public shaming of the 'offender'. The Elton Report offered a number of recommendations which are in stark contrast to this strategy. It states, for example, that 'Humiliating young people in front of their friends by, for example, public ridicule makes good relationships impossible. It breeds resentments which can poison the school's atmosphere' (p.101). Accordingly, the Report recommends that 'headteachers and teachers should avoid punishments which humiliate pupils' (R.27).

Creditably, Circular 8/94 amplifies Elton's advice, advising that 'individuals should not be made scapegoats for the activity of a class or group' and that 'punishments which are humiliating or degrading must not be used' (p.16). It is, therefore, somewhat depressing to note that, in a recently published book intended to support student teachers (Capel, Leask and Turner, 1995), the demeaning dogma of assertive discipline appears to be supported by the authors' recommendation of its training pack (p.118).

The use of drugs as a means of subduing aggressive or 'acting out' behaviours recalls the widespread preoccupation with electro-encephalograms (EEGs) in the 1950s and 1960s. Ritalin (methyl-phenidate) is the currently popular 'wonder drug', often used in cases where 'hyperactivity' (or, more fashionably, attention deficit disorder) has been 'diagnosed'. Teachers need to question the morality of such chemical interventions, for there can be little doubt that they may seriously compromise the rights of the child (and the professionalism of the teacher). O'Brien (1997) includes an account from a child aged 9: 'My tablets are to behave me. The thing is they don't behave me. It is me that behaves me not the tablets. I don't want teachers and my Mum to think its the tablet behaving me. I know another boy on the tablets – he's mad. I don't need them, I'm not mad like him, I want to be good'. The child is on the receiving-end of high-status, clinical diagnosis and categorisation and a management strategy which is cheap, easy to maintain and gives instant control to both teacher and parent. He has become, and will probably remain, a chemical child. The post-Elton era, in such cases, becomes highly selective about who should be accorded rights. And we have not even mentioned *Pindown...*

Conclusion

The nature and degree of success of educational responses to the Elton Report during the 1990s are symptomatic of the complex nature of the field it sought to address. In defining the nature of the problem the Report itself acknowledged the magnitude of the task (p.59), and it was quick to point out that 'Bad behaviour is not a new problem' and that 'Reducing bad behaviour is a realistic aim. Eliminating it completely is not' (p.65). The subsequent, and ongoing, struggle to find and develop appropriate responses will remain driven by the collective ideology of society and reacted to by the personal belief-systems of those most closely involved. There is evidence that many of the sensible recommendations contained in the Report, relating to every aspect of educational provision for pupils with problems, have been vigorously implemented in certain schools. It is at this level that the Elton Report has had its most impact, for, as has been suggested, more widespread solutions have been prejudiced by the general educational policies of the very government that conceived it.

Chapter 3

'The diameters of planets'
What makes an effective teacher of pupils with problems?

> ...teachers are made vulnerable to the effects of emotional disturbance in the child. The danger is then that in rejecting the behaviour, that the child is rejected. The teacher needs to make contact with the child in order to be able to teach the child at all, and he or she may be quite unprepared for the depths of hatred and rage in the child that can surge up (ILEA, 1985).

A popular perception of teachers who work with pupils with problems is that they are variously charismatic, oddball, liberal and divergent. My own experiences working in non-mainstream education has largely confirmed what has become something of an unfortunate Type-A stereotyping. Terry, for example, was a laconic, long-haired Art teacher, for whom the ILEA could offer no other opportunity than successive termly contracts in off-site units for so-called disruptive children. Terry fell, by accident, into his work with problem pupils as opportunity presented itself. He had no specific training before or during his many contracts. But this didn't make him an unsatisfactory teacher, far from it, the pupils he encountered felt attracted by his personality, by his ability to talk with enthusiasm about almost any topic, and by his caustic wit. Using these qualities to establish an appropriate mental set for working, Terry was able to encourage previously disaffected and unmotivated young people to perform at levels well beyond their expectations or those of their teachers.

More recently, in 1995, I encountered Louise, who was following several modules within Brunel University's professional development portfolio. Louise, too, had almost stumbled into work in a special school for children with EBD. She had worked for several years in a secondary school, then in a middle school. She decided to take a career break following the birth of her first child. Then, after '...giving a lot of thought to where I was going in my career and thinking that I'd like to try something a bit more challenging' (Louise, *verbatim* comment), she saw an advert for a part-time class-teacher in a local special school, and got the job. Like Terry, she had no formal training in EBD or associated needs, although some indication of her commitment to this area of work and to her own continuing professional development (CPD) is that she has undertaken to pay her own course fees – a regrettable feature of the parlous state of CPD funding.

Both cases lead us to ask important questions about the nature of professional activity with pupils with problems. Are there particular qualities and aptitudes which teachers need to possess to make meaningful contact with these children? If so, are such personal and professional attributes markedly different from the sets of competences identified by the Special Educational Needs Training Consortium (SENTC, 1996)? Both questions are fundamental to enhancing teaching and learning with this group of children. If there are no discernible differences – and some would argue that successful work with pupils with problems is mainly to do with a teacher's classroom management skills – then there seems to be little point in maintaining separate provision for such pupils. It has been widely acknowledged for years, for example, that those teachers who are effective with so-called ordinary children tend also to be effective with pupils who display more problematic behaviour (Kounin, 1966). What is the point then, one might well ask, of a specialist resource whose staff cannot acknowledge a set of discrete skills?

Some idea of the rather vague understanding of what these skills are can be gauged from Circular 9/94's less than helpful generalisation that 'Teachers who have come from ordinary schools to special schools will need further specialist training to help them develop the particular skills which will enable them to help children with emotional and behavioural difficulties' (DfE, 1994a. p.26). Quite apart from its tone of benevolent patronage, clearly rooted in Fulcher's (1990) discourse of charity, this statement provides the substantial part of the section in the Circular dealing with Staffing and in-service Training. Indeed, it could be argued that Circular 8/94 (DfE, 1994b) provides more in the way of guidelines for teachers working with pupils with problems *per se*. What we need to know, so that professional development pathways can be effectively plotted and supported, is what differentiates the specialist teacher of pupils with problems from those whose professional orientation lies mainly elsewhere.

The complexities inherent in working with pupils with problems ensure that determining a set of professional characteristics which prescribe the role is virtually impossible. Peagam (1995) acknowledges this, stating that '...the absence of a nationally validated, inter-professionally recognised qualification for teaching in this field can leave teachers feeling at the mercy of the 'expertise' that resides in other professions' (p.14). Significantly, Peagam observes that this contrasts markedly with the qualifications for teachers working with children with visual or hearing difficulties, which are based upon 'a body of theory and knowledge as the recognised basis for expertise'.

One of the crucial issues arising from this is the level of expertise required of those working with pupils with problems. Promoted posts in special education within mainstream schools are frequently advertised as requiring an additional qualification in special education; most usually this condition is satisfied by a diploma or masters degree with a general SEN specialism. Additional qualification is often sought in such areas of special education as autism, multi-sensory impairment and language and communication difficulties. As Cooper, Smith and Upton (1990) have indicated, however, only 30% of the teachers they surveyed in 133 schools and units held additional qualifications relating to working with children with EBD. Clearly, therefore, some response to

Smith's (1988) call for the development of a theoretical framework to underpin practice. Together with specific knowledge of a range of intervention techniques this ought to be something which comprises the basis for a taxonomy of professional attributes for teachers working in the field.

A recent attempt to provide such a framework, albeit in outline form only, was contained in the report of SENTC (1996). This provided a series of appendices which outlined sets of 'competencies' for different groups of teachers, according to the SEN area they were connected with (see Figure 1). I do not at this stage wish to rework the factional debate that mention of the term 'competency' brings with it; this has been undertaken elsewhere in respect of teacher education and special educational needs (Davies and Garner, 1997). But there are some issues which do merit attention in specific relation to teachers working with pupils with problems. The SENTC competencies were intended to focus on EBD, rather than on pupils with problems generally. On closer examination the list of competencies presents a major problem in that it does not set out a definable and distinct set of professional attributes. It is clear that each of the twelve items in the list are general descriptions only; it is fair to assume that this marked a first, tentative attempt to particularise what is the professional essence of working with EBD pupils. In order for them to be identifiers of a specialist professional workforce they need to be presented as a more finite and measurable set of characteristics. Some of the competences are what would be expected of a reasonably competent teacher working in a general mainstream classroom: the first 'competency' in the list is a case in point: is it too much to expect any teacher to have a 'knowledge and understanding of the factors within and outside schools that may influence the social, emotional, cognitive and behavioural development of pupils'? But, as we shall see, even those teachers most involved with pupils with problems find it difficult to identify the technical dimensions of their activity.

Generalisation is also the by-word of the OFSTED framework for the inspection of special schools (OFSTED, 1995a). The

Figure 1: Competencies Required by teachers of Children with Emotional and Behavioural Difficulties*

Context

1. knowledge and understanding of the factors within and outside schools that may influence the social, emotional, cognitive and behavioural development of pupils;

2. knowledge and understanding of psychological and biological factors which influence the emotional and social development of the pupil;

Curriculum Access and delivery

3. knowledge, skills and understanding to recognise when a social, emotional, learning and/or behavioural difficulty may require intervention involving: the target pupil's peers, other staff within the school, the family or the involvement of others outside the immediate classroom context;

4. knowledge, skills and understanding to assess and intervene to meet a pupils learning difficulty, taking into account the emotional and behavioural needs of the pupil;

5. knowledge, skills and understanding of a variety of assessment approaches to identify and analyse behaviour e.g. systematic observation schedules...

6. knowledge, skills and understanding of a variety of intervention approaches and the ability to monitor and evaluate their effectiveness in relation to an individual pupil e.g. behavioural intervention strategies, approaches derived from systemic family therapy in relation to conflict and its management, the 'person centred' approach of Carl Rogers

7. knowledge, skills and understanding of conflict management

8. knowledge, skills and understanding of therapeutic and cognitive strategies, where appropriate to help pupils to develop new ways of thinking and strategies that will enable them to behave differently and develop self-esteem;

Management

9. knowledge and understanding of the specific contribution that teachers can make to the multi-professional approach;

10. a knowledge and understanding of the role of consultation procedures with pupils, parents and colleagues in and out of school in meeting pupil need;

11. the knowledge, skills and understanding to achieve multi-professional cooperation and collaboration in the identification, assessment and response to social, emotional and behavioural problems;

12. a knowledge and understanding of practical and theoretical sources relating to these issues (i.e. literature on classroom management, effective teaching and learning, the identification and management of social, emotional and behavioural and learning difficulties).

* from SENTC (1996) *Professional Development to Meet Special Educational Needs*. Stafford: SENTC

document rightly focuses on curriculum matters in much of what it says is the 'quality of teaching' (p.68-75). But little of what is provided sets out a different inspection agenda to that provided in the documents relating to mainstream schools. Given the emphasis on defining inclusive approaches at the present time (see, for example, Thomas, 1998), this is hardly surprising. But if those teachers working with pupils with problems are to be assessed according to the same framework (more or less) as their mainstream counterparts, this appears both unfair and confusing. It is unfair, given that many pupils who have 'problems' provide perhaps the most daunting challenge of all within the spectrum of SEN. There needs to be some acknowledgement of this in the framework. Its absence makes for a confusing situation: are teachers who work with pupils with problems given additional salary allowances simply because, absorbing the effects of problematic behaviours, they are an educational variant of a UN peace-keeping force?

The inspection framework remains unhelpful in the task of distinguishing the particular characteristics of the special school teacher's role in managing behaviour (p.73). Whilst achieving levels of appropriate behaviour is the goal of all special schools, it is clear that, for those dealing with pupils with problems, this inspection focus has particular relevance. But there is nothing in the short entry which poses the question 'Do teachers manage pupils well and achieve high standards of discipline?' to delineate a special context, or the assessment of a particular range of skills.

It may be necessary to go beyond the official and quasi-official guidelines for help on what marks out the 'territory' of the teacher who works mainly with 'pupils with problems'. It is noteworthy that most commentators place as much emphasis upon the personal, as opposed to the professional, characteristics of teachers. Robertson (1989) provides an exemplar. Leaving aside the outmoded nature of much of the content (such as that section dealing with the function of 'Forceful, dominant behaviour' within a teaching and learning context), Robertson's twelve items for 'successful teaching' are as much about personal demeanour, interactional style and personality as they are about specific teaching skills. The former are far more open to subjective opinion and, as will be discussed later in this chapter, this may provide a very real opportunity to involve pupils with problems themselves in distinguishing the qualities of an effective teacher.

One of the dangers of such subjectivity, however, is that it can give rise to some sweeping assumptions about what it takes to be 'successful' with pupils with problems. Robertson (*op.cit.*) betrays this tendency when he states that 'The opportunity to watch experienced teachers is one which many students take advantage of... Observing how successful teachers cope in their first meetings with difficult classes can be very helpful' (p.148). Here there is an assumption that the crucial affective qualities relating to personal approaches to children are automatically obtained by experience. Some of the most deviance-provocative teachers are those older teachers whose cynicism of, and detachment from, the real experiences of young people ensure their continued incapacity to offer anything worthwhile to pupils with problems. It is doubtful that they would number amongst Woodhead's (mythical) 15,000.

Hargreaves (1975) also identifies the characteristics which make for effective teachers; those who have high expectations of all pupils, who assumed that pupils wished to cooperate and learn, and who signal by their actions both inside and outside the classroom that they like and respect pupils, irrespective of their reputation or previous performances. These themes were subsequently pursued by the Elton Report (1989).

The literature on school-effect and school effectiveness has had a dual impact on the potential creation of a composite and measurable set of teacher-attributes for working with pupils with problems. The work of Reynolds (1976), Rutter *et.al.* (1979), Mortimore *et.al.* and Reid *et.al.* (1986) has emphasised that schools and teachers have a significant effect on the behaviour of children. Contrary to current official attitudes about educational research, much of practical merit has come from such studies. On the debit side, however, the same studies have highlighted teachers themselves as causal factors in the problematic behaviour of some children. This was officially confirmed by HMI (1987).

The dilemma, therefore, in mapping a set of professional attributes in this field is that some teachers are part of the problem; in a profession which has become (in some ways justifiably) sensitive to criticism, such internal soul-searching runs contrary to the solidarity which is so frequently required. What is more, even the official statement by HMI on 'good behaviour and discipline' placed a heavy emphasis on subjective personal characteristics (such as 'warmth' and 'sensitivity') rather than a clearly itemised set of strategies and ways of working (HMI, *ibid.*).

It seems rather less than coincidental, therefore, that the most recent literature in EBD, pupils with problems and managing discipline (*sic*) in schools places discrete emphasis on the qualities required to work in this challenging arena. Cole, Visser and Uptons (1998) revealing account of contemporary provision and practice in EBD contains a chapter which explores the characteristics of teachers. Here some emphasis is given to the personal qualities of teachers, their rank ordering of these identifying 'consistency', 'fairness' and a 'sense of humour' as the most important. Blandford (1998), too, argues that teacher-personality should not be underestimated in managing the problematic behaviour of pupils. And O'Brien (1998) has some forthright views on what it takes to work in a 'battle zone' (*sic*). Each of these contributions to the literature, reveals a growing concern about what constitutes an appropriate repertoire for working with 'pupils with problems' – and infer that it is the personal characteristics of teachers which may be the key to successful interventions.

Give us a clue. Teachers' views on personal and professional characteristics

Sixty teachers, all of whom had some designated responsibility for 'pupils with problems', were randomly chosen from state primary, secondary and special schools in three Outer London boroughs and three county Local Education Authorities. The selection procedure used a sampling frame on a database of all schools within the six administrative areas. Two teachers from each school were invited to respond, after thier headteachers gave permission.

Each teacher was asked to complete an open-ended task, which required her to identify a set of personal and professional characteristics which, in her opinion, were most likely to equip teachers to work successfully with EBD pupils. The teachers were also asked to rank their selection according to importance (1 = most important, 2 = next most important, etc.). Three teachers were randomly selected from each phase to be interviewed using a semi-structured schedule developed in part from the data obtained from the whole cohort. The interview was designed to elicit teacher-views about the data itself: how did they feel, for example, that their professional activity appeared to be underpinned by personal (affective), rather than professional (technical) skills? The purpose of the whole exercise was to catalogue a set of clear, unambiguous and non-subjective teacher skills.

Details of the age, gender, training and current teaching post of the sample are provided in Figure 2. The data provides some basic structural information about the skewed profile of those working in the sector. A high percentage are women (70%), and over 75% have over ten years of teaching experience. Only two of these teachers (3%) had attended award-bearing long courses leading to an additional qualification relating to EBD; just over 16% of respondents had obtained an SEN qualification after their initial training. Almost half of the teachers (45%) had not attended an EBD-related professional development (short) course provided by a Local Education Authority or other provider. Each of these issues, whilst not directly relevant to a set of professional attributes, is worth further comment. The gender imbalance suggests either (a) that women may be more suited to this kind of teaching or (b) that it replicates the position in the rest of special education. Whilst some of the personal characteristics identified by the teachers in the sample are those which have been attributed to women – and perhaps enable them to function more effectively – there is little doubt that the traditional view of special education as a 'caring' profession still remains and that many male teachers do not regard this as 'real teaching'. The over-representation of older teachers has implications for the future. The negative publicity given to 'pupils with problems' (and, by association, to

FIGURE 2: Characteristics of Respondents (n = 60)
(*NB. Total presented first, then Primary / Secondary and Special School sub-total*)

Gender

M	18	(2	9	7)
F	42	(18	11	13)

Age

21-30	15	(7 6 1)
31-40	21	(6 6 9)
41-50	16	(4 7 5)
51+	6	(1 1 4)

Initial Qualifications

BEd	23	(14 4 5)
BA/BSc + QTS	3	(0 3 0)
1st Degree + PGCE	34	(10 16 8)

Post-Experience Qualifications

DPSE (EBD-specific)	1	(0 0 1)
DPSE (SEN)	4	(0 1 3)
MA/MEd (EBD-specific)	1	(0 0 1)
MA/MEd (SEN)	3	(1 1 1)
Other *	1	(0 0 1)

* *Diploma in Counselling*

Attendance on LEA or other 'short' EBD-related course (last 4 yrs)

More than 5	9	(1 2 6)
3-4	11	(2 3 6)
1-2	13	(2 2 9)

Current Role

SENCo	12	(4 8 0)
Class/Subject teacher	34	(11 9 14)
Deputy Headteacher	6	(2 1 3)
Support Teacher	4	(1 2 1)
Part-Time Teacher	4	(2 1 1)

teachers who work with them), together with the nakedness of SEN input in initial teacher education courses (Garner, 1996), a crisis in supply of experienced teachers may be awaiting the EBD sector. The low percentage of teachers who have amplified their practice by attending additional courses of training since qualification may in itself signal a perception that working with EBD children requires no additional technical skills.

The professional and personal attributes which this set of teachers felt were the most important are itemised in Figure 3. What is clear from these prioritised lists is that the teachers found it very difficult to separate the professional (i.e. technical) characteristics of doing their job from those of a more personal (i.e. affective) nature. The list of professional attributes provided by these teachers is remarkable in that it remains at the level of generality in most instances. Communication skills, besides being the most frequently mentioned characteristic, was rated most important (23% of teachers). Skills with individual pupils was positioned first by 14% of the teachers, whilst classroom management was selected by 11%.

Each of these named characteristics is highly unspecific as to the knowledge, skills and techniques that they encompass. Few of the teachers provided detailed responses. The term 'communication skills' has been adopted as a blanket term to cover such response-items as 'communication with other professionals', 'listening skills' and 'non-verbal communication'. Similarly, 'individual skills' was used to accommodate a spectrum of responses which included 'prioritising behaviour', 'writing IEPs' and 'use of rewards and sanctions'. And 'classroom management' incorporated such things as 'organisational skills' and 'keeping the children on task'.

Moreover, each of the three most frequently mentioned attributes replicate much of the tone, if not the substance, of the statutory guidelines currently in place for the training of teachers (DfEE, 1997). Circular 10/97 includes an emphasis on each of these in its Requirements for Courses of Initial Teacher Training, noting that, for the award of Qualified Teacher Status (QTS), students must be

FIGURE 3: Personal and Professional Attributes of Teachers

Professional Characteristics (total mentions)

Communication Skills	37
Classroom Management Skills	29
Skills with individual pupils	29
Additional qualifications/experience	18
Reflection on practice	15
Knowledge of causes	15
Knowledge of support systems	9
Needs of EBD pupils	6
Subject Knowledge	4
Miscellaneous	19

Total choices = 181

Personal Characteristics (total mentions)

Humour	46
Patience	39
Calmness	29
Empathy	27
Consistency	24
Sociability	18
Creative	13
Communication Skills	12
Fairness	9
Miscellaneous	17

Total choices = 242

Personal and Professional Characteristics Combined (total mentions)

Humour	46
Patience	39
Communication Skills	37
Classroom Management Skills	29
Skills with individual pupils	29
Calmness	29
Empathy	27
Consistency	24
Sociability	18
Additional qualifications/experience	18

FIGURE 3: Personal and Professional Attributes of Teachers (continued)

Professional Characteristics (% top priority)

Communication Skills	23
Classroom Management Skills	14
Skills with individual pupils	11
Additional qualifications/experience	10
Reflection on practice	10
Knowledge of causes	9
Knowledge of support systems	6
Needs of EBD pupils	5
Subject Knowledge	3
Miscellaneous	9

Personal Characteristics (% top priority)

Humour	32
Patience	24
Calmness	16
Empathy	11
Consistency	7
Sociability	4
Creative	2
Communication Skills	2
Fairness	2
Miscellaneous	0

Personal and Professional Characteristics Combined (% top priority)

Humour	32
Patience	24
Communication Skills	23
Calmness	16
Classroom Management Skills	14
Empathy	11
Skills with individual pupils	11
Additional qualifications/experience	10
Reflection on practice	10
Knowledge of causes	9

able to demonstrate 'clear instruction and demonstration... effective questioning... listening carefully to pupils' (i.e. communication skills), 'effective teaching... of individuals... matching the approaches used to... the pupils being taught' (i.e. skills with individual pupils) and to 'establish and maintain a purposeful working atmosphere... (and)... set high expectations for pupils' behaviour' (i.e. classroom management).

The same attributes are also fundamental to the prevailing school inspection framework for primary schools, for example (Ofsted, 1996b), whilst there is little contained in the parallel document relating to special schools to demonstrate a teacher's duties for these establishments, as has been pointed out earlier in this chapter.

The teachers participating in this study appeared more at home when providing their views on what constituted personal attributes – it is noteworthy that this part of the exercise elicited 242 responses against only 181 responses for the professional characteristics category. The use of humour was rated the most important attribute, both in terms of frequency and its position as the top priority: 32% of the teachers rating it first. 'Patience' also outscored the most frequently mentioned professional characteristic, and was ranked top by 24% of the teachers, whilst 'calmness' (16%) and 'empathy' (11%) also scored highly as first choices.

If the two sets of attributes are viewed as a composite it becomes clear that personal characteristics outscore professional attributes in terms of total numbers of mentions. It is important not to underestimate the importance of personal attributes of teachers, as so-called disruptive pupils pointedly illustrate (Garner, 1993). Nevertheless it is obvious to anyone involved in education that these are characteristics which are problematic in their subjectivity, their variation from one person to the next, and to their lack of measurability. At a time when teachers are officially evaluated (mainly) according to sets of quantifiable criteria, the absence of a clearly stated taxonomy of skills for teachers working with pupils with problems may be possibly limiting, even damaging, to the teachers involved. Some indication of the concerns that teachers have about this situation is provided in the interviews which accompanied this study.

When a small sample of the cohort were interviewed each of the teachers expressed some surprise, and concern, that there did not appear to a set of identifiable, and measurable, professional skills which prescribed their role with pupils with problems. At the same time, however, each of the teachers involved vigorously defended the notions of interpersonal skills, relationship-building and empathy (to give some examples of personal characteristics) as being inherently 'professional'. Tom provided an initial response to the data-set by stating that 'It makes me look like a child-minder, doesn't it?', later going on to confess that 'I think we sometimes try to justify the work we do on other peoples' terms, not on our own'. The latter remark is very telling, and indicates the dilemmas facing those with experience of pupils with problems: we know that the work is different, and that the children have highly individual, often personal, needs. And yet there is an abiding desire to have the respect of colleagues who operate with so-called 'ordinary' children (though I hesitate to use such a pejorative term). Harriet describes this situation as '...like having two masters or trying to win two races' and believes that '...the only way to gain respect is to build up a list of skills that we have and then describe them in real terms relating to the classroom'. Without this, according to June, '...we are in danger of being seen as the old-fashioned, do-gooding person who just loves kids to death'.

Irrespective of the possible methodological shortcomings of its collection, this data provides us with some important clues surrounding (a) what it takes to be a teacher who works mainly with pupils with problems and (b) the implications for continuing professional development. The first issue relates to the nature of professionalism, with particular regard to the relationship between education and therapy. The second has implications for the maintenance of high-standard teaching and learning with what is a large number of the school-age population.

In the case of teacher-professionalism it is possible to argue, as Halliday (1996) has done, that 'Teachers are already members of such traditions through their professional knowledge as geographers, physicists and most especially teachers. It is foolish to ignore this professionalism... professionalism cannot be divorced from non-professional concerns' (p.5). He believes that '...there is no point in specifying something that cannot practically be checked', implying that teaching should remain at a level of 'professional artistry'. Unfortunately it is not possible to maintain any substantive position within the education service by adopting such a head-in-the-sand ideology. We can *privately* think that what we do within the affective domain is as important as that in the more substantive formal curriculum, but few would survive the sledgehammer scrutiny of OFSTED by adopting such an approach.

Moreover, the mapping of a set of technical components which underpin work with pupils with problems is central to the task of defining a framework for continuing professional development. CPD in special education is problematic in terms of its structure, content and the way it is currently funded (or not funded...) as has been recently pointed out (SENTC, *op.cit.*; Davies and Garner, *op.cit.*). At the present time the Teacher Training Agency (TTA) has controversially identified sets of providers of in-service training (*sic*), based upon submissions from institutions of higher education (IHEs) and others. Proposals had to demonstrate the relevance to teachers of course content for predetermined outcomes. These have to be described in terms that can be measured. It would seem unlikely that the TTA would countenance course proposals aimed to '...make teachers more humorous'...

This is not to trivialise the dilemma for providers (or the recipients of such courses). In the CPD market place, those responsible for pupils with problems have to seek funds for professional advancement in competition with other teachers. The years since 1988 have seen high proportions of in-service funds being directed to National Curriculum subject-content and its assessment, recording and reporting. Both areas can be conceptually and structurally ring-fenced. This makes them easier to define in the kind of TTA *input-output* speak that will secure them funding. CPD providers who devise generic courses for teachers working with pupils with problems may need to adopt a pragmatic approach in respect of content should they wish to continue on the Agency's 'A' list...

The Schools Minister has given notice that new regulations for the appraisal of teachers will be brought into force in September, 1999 (Morris, 1998). In announcing this she has declared that 'Appraisal is about enabling teachers to be effective professionals and about developing their knowledge and skills in a focused way'. There was also an accompanying statement which indicated that 'We shall be undertaking wide-ranging consultation prior to bringing new regulations into force'. The two statements serve as warning to those working with pupils with problems, that they need to begin the task of defining those discrete elements of their practice which prescribe their professionalism.

There are some blunt indications from the small-scale study supporting this chapter that the teachers themselves recognise personal attributes more readily, and prioritise them highly as prerequisites for effective work with pupils with problems. Rather than have a professional development agenda dictated from 'outside', therefore, it seems essential that provider and consumer decide on a set of content characteristics for serving teachers. In this context, attention to balance between theory and practice will do much to ensure the 'professional' status of teachers who work with pupils with problems. In attempting to achieve this it is important to recognise Samuel Johnson's dictum that 'You teach your daughters the diameters of planets, and wonder what you have done that they do not delight in your company' (*Miscellanies*, Volume 1). Put more simply, a major challenge facing teachers who work with children who present emotional and/or behavioural difficulties will be to define those characteristics of teachers which create the conditions for successful intervention: as Cole and Visser (1998) have inferred, these are as much about intuition and creativity as they are about curriculum input and classroom management.

Chapter 4

Establishing Ownership
the rhetoric and realities of
whole-school approaches

The 1990s have seen a significant rise of awareness to the possi-
bilities of inclusive education. Though the concept is scarcely new,
with Thomas, Walker and Webb (1998) tracing its historical
origins to the work of Burgwin and other social activists in the
early 19th century, its application as a policy initiative in education and social care in England and Wales can be located in the
recommendations of the Warnock Report (1978). The development of 'integrationist' approaches in special education subsequent to that Report and the 1981 and 1983 legislation which
implemented its findings have been an important initiative in
mainstream practice.

But the development of more widespread inclusive practice in
England and Wales has been inhibited by a parochial attitude to
special education. This has meant that evidence of success elsewhere (notably in North America and certain parts of Western
Europe), has frequently gone unacknowledged. Moreover, the
efficacy of inclusion has not been unconditionally accepted, with
certain groups arguing that the needs of some children are best met
by segregated provision. Predictably the group most commonly
associated with the need to maintain separate schools and units are
pupils whose educational difficulties relate to their perceived
emotional and behavioural difficulties.

Nevertheless, the challenge to the orthodoxy of segregation,
which Pijl and Meijer (1994) regarded as being widely supported
in Western Europe, has been dramatic and has gathered pace dur-

ing the last twenty years. Though it is difficult to gauge the impact of international agreements on policy decisions taken within national systems, the UN Convention on the Rights of the Child (1989) and the Salamanca Statement (1994) showed an intention to focus on individual rights within education and welfare. The former sought to promote the inclusion of the child's view on educational and social matters (see Chapter 8), whilst the Salamanca Statement was '...arguably the most significant inter-national document that has ever appeared in the special needs field' stating that '...regular schools with an inclusive orientation are 'the most effective means of combating discriminatory atti-tudes, building an inclusive society and achieving education for all' ' (Ainscow, 1997, p.182). The two sets of resolutions provided an international context for a national policy agenda.

In England and Wales matters were taken forward in part by acci-dent but predominantly by design. I have already mentioned the importance of integrationist legislation in the 1980s, the relative merits and impact of which have been fully considered elsewhere (Hall, 1997). Although the negative effects of the 1988 Education Act have been well-documented (Bash and Coulby, 1989), the implementation of a National Curriculum following that Act gave, at least in principle, all children access to a uniform 'broad and balanced' curriculum. Whilst there are many persuasive contrary arguments (Fletcher-Campbell, 1996), an overall view, summarised by Lewis (1996), is that the initiative has had the beneficial effect of assisting the movement towards inclusive schooling.

The Code of Practice (DfE, 1994), too, carried some important messages regarding inclusion. Its guidance concerning 'Stage 1' of the identification, assessment and intervention process is a case in point. The Code specified that class-teachers (primary) or subject teachers (secondary) should be the vanguard agents of interven-tion with children with learning difficulties. Although such prac-tices were already common in many schools, the Code of Practice made them explicit, thereby throwing down a challenge to all teachers, and especially those who previously regarded such actions as the exclusive responsibility of SEN staff.

Confirmation of the centrality of inclusive approaches in educational policy-making in England and Wales was finally provided by the announcement of the Green Paper, *Excellence for All Children* (DfEE, 1997). It stated that 'We aim to increase the level and quality of inclusion within mainstream schools' so that, over the next five years, 'a growing number of mainstream schools will be willing and able to accept children with a range of SEN'.

I want to move away from a general discussion of inclusion, to focus upon the 'willing and able' conditions presented in the Green Paper and to look at them in the context of whole-school policies and the inclusion of children whose behaviour is problematic. In spite of some excellent examples of practice (see Thomas *et.al., op.cit.,* Sebba and Sachdev, 1997), there is a real danger that a policy vacuum concerning the inclusion of pupils with problems is being created. There is a dual significance, in this respect, that children with emotional and behavioural difficulties are the only group from the full range of learning difficulties to have been mentioned by name in the Green Paper, having assumed sufficient notoriety to have a full section of the Paper devoted to them. Firstly, there is the inference that, of all SENs, this is likely to remain the most controversial in terms of inclusion. Recent comments from representatives of teacher-unions bear this out (see Chapter 7), as does Thomas's *et al.* honest remark that '...children with physical difficulties were acceptable, but (that) more disruptive children...would cause problems' (p.122). But, secondly, the section of the Green Paper dedicated to EBD does not make the same explicit claims that inclusion is to be the main policy thrust with regard to this aspect of SEN. By hint of omission the official view, perhaps based on pragmatism, seems to have an exclusionary ring about it.

To avoid this becoming a reality, and to ensure that mainstream schools can be effective in their work with pupils with problems (including those who are statemented) a fundamental shift needs to be forthcoming in the way policy matters are discussed and implemented in schools. It should be understood that policy in this respect relates only in part to policies concerning behaviour or discipline. HMI (1987), for example, refer exclusively to behaviour policies when stating that these should '...have been worked out cooperatively and command the assent of all teachers' (p.4). And whilst most official recipes for 'success' since the Education Act (1988) have mentioned 'the involvement of pupils' (DES, 1989; DfE, 1994), they focus on matters relating to the regulation of problem behaviour, thus betraying a deficit-view of the pupils themselves.

What is needed is a 'holistic' strategy, providing a synthesis of all aspects of school life and relating each of them to the needs of pupils with problems – such 'ecosystemic' thinking relates to curriculum, social behaviour, school organisation, professional development, equality of opportunity, home-school links and so on. Every policy, code, procedure or working arrangement in a school should, in other words, be framed and belong to an ecosystemic whole. If pupils with problems are being picked out as 'special', in that they require a dedicated policy focus (and let us not forget that this is the group of pupils that a whole-school behaviour policy is *really* aimed at and has most impact on), then there should be more substantial consideration given to the way in which all other policies map out the schools' engagement with them. This position, in its ideal form, is one of policy-cohesiveness and policy-inclusiveness. In the absence of an official under-standing or explication of this policy-synergy, schools need actively to take the matter forward.

What we are talking about here is neither easy to grasp, nor to maintain. But there are a number of signposts which might be helpful. Nor should it go unrecognised that the development of the holistic policy for pupils with problems is unlikely to be a short term affair. One of the major reasons for the lack of innovation in schools has been the short-termism induced by the threat of external inspection. As the kind of approach mapped in this chapter is about an incremental, strategic approach to pupils with problems via the concept of the 'questioning school' (Mongon and Hart, 1989), there are risks to be taken and old taboos and prejudices to be confronted. Only by taking such steps will schools move away from reinventing strategies that half-work, are rhetoric-laden and which affect only the mostly bid-dable pupils anyway.

Thankfully there is a developing body of literature concerning alternative ways of working with pupils with problems, and with the principles of inclusion – some of this material is referred to at various other points in this book. Sebba and Sachdev (*op.cit.*), for example, are careful to provide both a set of potential benefits of inclusive practice and, reassuringly, to present exemplars of these in relation to pupils with problems. One crucial message under-lying these is that schools need to question the extent to which inclusion is promoted by its policy relating to '...ethos, principles, admissions, curriculum, teaching, support, use of resources, assessment and accreditation, parental involvement and links with the community' (p.35). In other words, there is no specific mention of a 'behaviour policy', implying that isolating matters concerning behaviour from other aspects of school life may result in the policy itself being used as a scapegoating mechanism.

Underlying any attempt to refine and reorientate whole-school policy along the lines suggested above is a key question: 'Who has the control?' This can be supplemented by a secondary question 'Is everybody happy about the status quo?' Both questions need answers before embarking on policies-reformulation.

The pre-1988 response to the first question would be that it is the classroom teacher who is very much in control. She made deci-sions about what was taught, how it was taught, and how even-tually assessed; the most significant standardisation required being that of the school itself and its chosen procedures and prac-tices. Once the classroom door was closed the teacher was, for better or worse, Queen of that territory: a knock on the door by the visitor was more than a symbolic courtesy – it was an entry visa into the private world of the classroom. In matters of dis-cipline, the same territoriality obtained, with individual teachers frequently adopting idiosyncratic sanctions when pupils mis-behaved. This hierarchical approach was manifest in the teacher's interactional style. As Charlton (1996) maintains, '...teachers also appear to practise extensive control in their domination of class-room discourse. Although talk is common in classrooms, teachers seem to monopolise 70 per cent of it' (p.37).

The teacher's weakening control over what went on in classrooms was signalled by the 1988 Education Act. For the first time since the Revised Code in the nineteenth century teachers had to work according to a prescribed curriculum; even worse, they had virtually no say in how it was constructed. Similar controls over assessment were introduced at the same time, which arguably emasculated teachers still further. But the 1988 Act impacted in even more dramatic ways on pedagogy. New arrangements for school inspection meant that even teaching style was to be subject to draconian scrutiny, with the likelihood of punitive outcomes for individual teachers and whole schools whose practice was viewed as unsatisfactory. This may also include those teachers who choose to work in non-conventional or alternative ways with pupils with problems.

These changes to the basic procedures, structures and understandings of teaching have brought with them increased bureaucracy, a decrease in the time available for teachers to interact with pupils, and a rule-governed approach to curriculum delivery. Such a dramatic change in philosophy and operational style requires that schools, if they are to develop the kinds of radical and holistic approaches for pupils with problems mentioned above, engage reflectively with a broad range of interdependent themes. These would crucially relate to:

- how the school as an institution sees itself and the work it does in relation to pupils (with problems)

- what are the real and perceived barriers to learning for pupils (with problems)

- what are the range of teaching and learning interventions utilised by teachers of pupils with problems and

- what procedures are adopted across the whole school for the shared management of the difficulties encountered and presented by pupils with problems.

Such questions (and there are many others, some of which will be highly context-dependent), taken incrementally, could lead to a more effective whole-school dimension for all participants, notably for those young people whose behaviour is a cause for concern. The remainder of this chapter considers one small-scale example of the kind of local enquiry which, if used as a strategic data-gathering device in a single school, can help highlight and expose the often sharp differences in perception as to 'what works' with pupils with problems.

Asking questions: do 'contracts' work?

Schools reflect the beliefs, perceptions, motives and objectives of many individuals. They are influenced by what goes on both in the school and outside. Legislation introduced since 1988 plus the acknowledgment that school populations have been influenced by significant changes in society, have placed the ethos or 'climate' of schools at the epicentre of the battle to win the hearts of pupils with problems. Previous analyses of this phenomenon have enhanced our understanding of its special importance for pupils with problems (Hargreaves, 1967; Lacey, 1970; Willis, 1977; Rutter, *et al.*, 1979; Everhart, 1983).

More recently, McManus (1995) summarised the impact of a 'school's organisational ethos, distribution of authority, systems of appraisal, as well as the rewards offered...' as influencing '...the perceptions, decisions and actions – whether to comply, disengage or rebel' (p.126). Cooper and McIntyre (1996), too, provide a sobering reminder that '...the individual teacher's task is made more difficult if there is not a school climate in which all individuals are consistently treated with respect', indicating that fostering a positive, pupil-centred ethos ultimately benefits teachers too. So, even though painful soul-searching is the order of the day, there are huge benefits to be accrued for all.

A starting point for this may be to investigate the attitudes and beliefs of all staff, in order to establish a context. In justifying such an exercise, as a starting point for the inclusion of pupils with problems within mainstream schools, the previously acknowledged work by Sebba and Sachdev (*op.cit.*) and Thomas and Webb, *op.cit.*) is thought-provoking. All teachers should, as part of their day-to-day routines, be exposed to this kind of material. Thus familiarity with current critical reflection (as opposed to statutory guidance) should be the first step towards the creation of a thinking school on matters of holistic policy and inclusion.

Education may have absorbed too much financially-orientated jargon in recent years, yet the use of an 'audit' here does seem appropriate. These have become an accepted way of assessing the current status of a given approach, topic or body of opinion, and their use in schools is now widespread (Drakeford, 1997; Williams, 1996). Crucially, however, they must agree unilaterally that further investigation and discussion is required in the first place. Above all, the senior management of a school needs to recognise a possible lack of policy-cohesiveness and policy-inclusiveness with regard to pupils with problems. This could be a major stumbling block, highlighting the need for a focus upon pupils within the new training arrangements for headteachers. Although these matters have relevance to all schools, it is frequently the school which is regarded as in danger of 'failing' that may be in need of the most dynamic policy-reorientation of all. But these are often the most resistant to change, for, as Reynolds (1989) points out 'Threatened or insecure staff groups are, in my experience, the least likely to take up any form of in-service exercise' (p.38).

I am going to illustrate the importance of enquiry by the use made by schools of 'contracts'. Behaviour contracts have been used for many years as a strategy to help ameliorate unwanted behaviours in children in schools in England and Wales (Burland, 1979; West-macott and Cameron, 1981). They have been described as comprising '...an agreement between two or more parties that sets down the responsibilities of the parties concerning a particular activity that will lead to the achieving of specific target behaviours' (Ayers, Clarke and Murray, 1995). Elsewhere, Stuart (1971) summarised contracts, used in the context of modifying behaviour, as having '...the effect of structuring reciprocal exchanges. They specify who is to do what, for whom, under what circumstances'.

Interest in the use of formal 'contracts' relating to behaviour has, in recent years, become widespread (McNamara, 1987; Gillborn, Nixon and Ruddock, 1993; Fletcher and Presland, 1990). Most recently the Department for Education and Employment (DfEE) has requested responses to their suggestion that all schools put in place a 'home-school contract' (DfEE, 1997); whilst not explicitly, or solely, relating to the management of behaviour, this initiative is indicative of the intention to establish a (quasi-) legal basis for their interactions with parents and pupils. Many schools have enthusiastically adopted this approach, in the face of such exhortations from central government; it has particularly been seen as an effective way of working with pupils with problems. But is it?.

Behaviour contracts show considerable variation in both construction and use. They can form an implicit part of a whole-school 'code of conduct', applied generally to all pupils on the school's roll. More specifically, an increasingly popular variant is that of the use of sets of class 'rules' on acceptable behaviour. In primary schools it is more common for informal contracting to occur, with the use of personal 'star charts' or other graphic devices (Roffey and O'Reirdan, 1997). However, it is the adoption of behaviour contracts *per se* for a particular set of pupils – those who are viewed as having SENs relating to their inability to behave in a manner appropriate to the standards set by the school – which is the central focus of this paper.

The effective use of contracts requires certain conditions to be met (Ayers, Clarke and Murray, *op.cit.*). Amongst these are that

- the contract must be realistic and fair
- it must focus on positive behavioural outcomes (i.e. it must be able to contribute to change in pupil behaviour)
- it must be written in language which is clear and un-ambiguous (iv) it must involve pupils, parents and teachers in its construction and use (in other words, it is not just the pupil who has 'contractual responsibilities'!)
- it must have a means by which it can be reviewed and evaluated.

These characteristics formed part of a questionnaire and interview schedule which I recently constructed; its purpose was to gauge the effectiveness of behaviour contracts from the point of view of teachers *and* pupils.

In spite of the range of theoretical recommendations as to what constitutes a 'good' behaviour contract, there has previously been little attempt to evaluate their effectiveness. Kinder and Wilkin (1996), for example, in their study of effective school-based strategies to deal with disaffection, make only one mention of the term – indicative, perhaps, of the paucity of evaluatory evidence. Given that behaviour contracts are now in widespread use in primary, secondary and special schools, and that their use has been officially sanctioned, the absence of evidence represents a serious oversight. New aircraft are not allowed to take to the air before their design and reliability have been thoroughly established in proving trials...

Gathering some data

In order to find out more about the role of contracts I picked at random eight schools (four secondary and four 'EBD' special schools), located in Greater London boroughs and their adjacent county LEAs. These were selected from returns to a letter which asked whether a school made use of written agreements or contracts as part of its behaviour policy: a hundred letters were distributed in this initial enquiry, and a response rate of 84% was obtained. In the second stage the headteacher of each of the eight selected schools was approached, requesting permission:

* to conduct a brief questionnaire survey of all pupils in Years 8 and 9 who had been placed at either Stage 2 or Stage 3 of the Code of Practice on account of their 'problem behaviour' (In the case of the special schools, a random sample of four Year 8 or 9 pupils from each school completed the questionnaire)

* to interview the teachers of pupils in the sample groups, concerning their views about the effectiveness of behaviour contracts and, finally

- to interview a random selection of the respondents in Years 8 and 9. In all 64 pupils (41 Secondary and 23 Special) and 22 teachers were involved in the survey. Sixteen pupils were subsequently interviewed.

Each pupil-interview utilised a semi-structured format. Interviews were recorded and then transcribed, the original tape being returned to the interviewee. In all cases parental permission was obtained and all respondents were given the opportunity to review their comments, on the understanding that anything they disagreed with could be amended or struck from the research record. In subsequent data-extracts all real names, of pupils, teachers and schools, have been disguised to ensure confidentiality.

In addition to this data, and as a means of illustrating and validating the pupils' responses, each school was asked to supply, in confidence, an example of the kind of behaviour contract they used. This documentary evidence was used in conjunction with the responses of the teachers from the schools to assess the pupils' views; the substance of the present paper principally concerns the latter.

Both the questionnaire and the semi-structured interview schedule, each comprising twelve questions, were organised around three aspects of behaviour contracts: their planning and organisation, their day-to-day use and their perceived effectiveness in helping to change, or curtail, unwanted behaviours. Some differentiation in language was introduced in those cases where a pupil was noted as having reading difficulties and provision was made for two children to audio-record their questionnaire response because of their poor handwriting skills.

Individual schools were identified only by letters (A-D for secondary schools, E-H for special schools). For the purpose of analysis and reporting individual pupils were numbered from 1-41 (secondary schools) and 42-64 (special schools); teachers were numbered 65-87. In this chapter, and as an illustration of the use that a questioning school can make of pupils as a resource, I concentrate mainly on their views rather than those expressed by their teachers. A summary of the data obtained is provided in Figures 4-6.

Pupils' views on contracts and agreements

Only four female pupils were represented in this sample, supporting a traditional view that boys, rather than girls, are inclined to engage in inappropriate behaviour (Crozier and Anstiss, 1996). All the pupils surveyed in this study had, at some stage in their school career, been the subject of, or participated in, a contract or agreement. One respondent (E47) recalled being thus involved on 'about ten or twelve times'; more usually, however, the pupils reported that the number of occasions in which they were involved in this kind of procedure was three to five.

All the schools in the sample used 'contracts' or 'agreements' with pupils as an integral part of their behaviour management policy. Two of the special schools in the study routinely placed every pupil on a contract, reviewed at monthly intervals. In this respect both schools were using the contract as a pre-emptive device, rather than as a response to a specific event or series of incidents. All eight made specific mention of the use of some form of contract or agreement in their written policy on discipline, and included a description of the process (in greater or less detail) in the information distributed to parents and carers.

When questioned about the reasons why they had been placed on a contract the pupils provided a diverse list. The most frequent mentions were of 'disobedience' to particular teachers (45%), (school) rule-breaking (38%) and unauthorised absences from school (22%). Aggressive or violent conduct was infrequently mentioned (9%), although bullying (of younger pupils) was indicated as a factor by three pupils. From the interview data it became apparent that there was no set procedure for the introduction of a contract: some pupils reported being placed on a contract after a single incident, whilst others implied that this occurred after a series of incidents over a longer period. Finally, a number of pupils (nine) inferred that they were the recipient of a contract because their teachers '...didn't like them' (e.g. B23).

FIGURE 4: MAINSTREAM (SECONDARY) and SPECIAL (COMPOSITE DATA)

Do you think that a written agreement or contract between you and your teacher would help you to work harder or better?

Learning: YES (27)   NO (23)   DON'T KNOW (14)
Behaviour: YES (41)   NO (18)   DON'T KNOW (5)

Did your teachers and parents, as well as you, have to do things within the agreement?

Teachers: YES (14)   NO (32)   DON'T KNOW (18)
Parents: YES (26)   NO (30)   DON'T KNOW (8)

How many 'rules' do/did you have to keep?

1-2 (9)   3-5 (32)   5+ (17)   DON'T KNOW (6)

Who decides the content of the contract or agreement?

Teachers Only (21) Pupils Only (0) Teachers and Pupils (17) Parents and Teachers (7) Teachers, Parents and Pupils (13) Don't Know (6)

Did you know it was going to be used?
YES (39)   NO (14)   DON'T KNOW (11)

Who makes sure that you keep to the agreement?
Named Teacher (26) Head/Deputy (16) Teachers and Parents (5)
Teachers, Parents and Pupil (10)
Don't Know (7)

How frequently do you discuss it with your teacher(s)
Each Day (6)   Each Week (27)   Every 2-3 weeks (18)   Longer (13)

Did your classmates or friends know anything about it?
YES (26)   NO (31)   DON'T KNOW (7)

Did having a contract make you feel: special (7), more important (2) different (10) sorry (5) punished (19) Don't know (14)

Did your parents know about it?
YES (36)   NO (24)   DON'T KNOW (4)

Were they involved in setting it up?
YES (17)   NO (34)   DON'T KNOW (13)

Do they help you to keep to the contract?
YES (29)   NO (15)   SOMETIMES (10) DON'T KNOW (10)

Did your teachers talk to you about it?
YES (29)   NO (31)   DON'T KNOW (4)

Do your teachers help you to keep the contract?
YES (23)   NO (37)   DON'T KNOW (4)

Has their attitude to you changed?
YES (16)   NO (33)   DON'T KNOW (15)

FIGURE 5: MAINSTREAM DATA

Do you think that a written agreement or contract between you and your teacher would help you to work harder or better?

Learning: YES (11)   NO (16)   DON'T KNOW (14)
Behaviour: YES (21)   NO (16)   DON'T KNOW (4)

Did your teachers and parents, as well as you, have to do things within the agreement?
Teachers: YES (5)   NO (21)   DON'T KNOW (15)
Parents: YES (10)   NO (25)   DON'T KNOW (6)

How many 'rules' do/did you have to keep?

1-2 (2)   3-5 (20)   5+ (15)   DON'T KNOW (6)

Who decides the content of the contract or agreement?
Teachers Only (18) Pupils Only (0) Teachers and Pupils (6) Parents and Teachers (6) Teachers, Parents and Pupils (6) Don't Know (5)

Did you know it was going to be used?
YES (21)   NO (12)   DON'T KNOW (8)

Who makes sure that you keep to the agreement?
Named Teacher (16) Head/Deputy (12) Teachers and Parents (4) Teachers, Parents and Pupil (2)
Don't Know (7)

How frequently do you discuss it with your teacher(s)?
Each Day (0)   Each Week (10)   Every 2-3 weeks (18)   Longer (13)

Did your classmates or friends know anything about it?
YES (10)   NO (24)   DON'T KNOW (7)

Did having a contract make you feel: special (0) more important (2) different (6) sorry (2) punished (14) Don't Know (17))

Did your parents know about it?
YES (20)   NO (20)   DON'T KNOW (1)

Were they involved in setting it up?
YES (7)   NO (27)   DON'T KNOW (7)

Do they help you to keep to the contract?
YES (13)   NO (12)   SOMETIMES (8)   DON'T KNOW (8)

Did your teachers talk to you about it?
YES (13)   NO (26)   DON'T KNOW (2)

Do your teachers help you to keep the contract?
YES (5)   NO (33)   DON'T KNOW (3)

Has their attitude to you changed?
YES (10)   NO (17)   DON'T KNOW (14)

FIGURE 6: SPECIAL SCHOOL DATA

Do you think that a written agreement or contract between you and your teacher would help you to work harder or better?

Learning: YES (16)   NO (7)   DON'T KNOW (0)
Behaviour: YES (20)   NO (2)   DON'T KNOW (1)

Did your teachers and parents, as well as you, have to do things within the agreement?

Teachers: YES (9)   NO (11)   DON'T KNOW (3)
Parents: YES (16)   NO (5)   DON'T KNOW (2)

How many 'rules' do/did you have to keep?

1-2 (9)   3-5 (12)   5+ (2)   DON'T KNOW (0)

Who decides the content of the contract or agreement?

Teachers Only (3) Pupils Only (0) Teachers and Pupils (11) Parents and Teachers (1) Teachers, Parents and Pupils (7) Don't Know (1)

Did you know it was going to be used?

YES (18)   NO (2)   DON'T KNOW (3)

Who makes sure that you keep to the agreement?

Named Teacher (10) Head/Deputy (4) Teachers and Parents (1) Teachers, Parents and Pupil (8) Don't Know (0)

How frequently do you discuss it with your teacher(s)?

Each Day (6)   Each Week (17)   Every 2-3 weeks (0)   Longer (0)

Did your classmates or friends know anything about it?

YES (16)   NO (7)   DON'T KNOW (0)

Did having a contract make you feel: special (7) more important (0) different (4) sorry (1) punished (4) Don't Know (7))

Did your parents know about it?

YES (16)   NO (4)   DON'T KNOW (3)

Were they involved in setting it up?

YES (10)   NO (7)   DON'T KNOW (6)

Do they help you to keep to the contract?

YES (16)   NO (3)   SOMETIMES (2)   DON'T KNOW (2)

Did your teachers talk to you about it?

YES (16)   NO (5)   DON'T KNOW (3)

Do your teachers help you to keep the contract?

YES (18)   NO (4)   DON'T KNOW (1)

Has their attitude to you changed?

YES (6)   NO (16)   DON'T KNOW (1)

The data suggested that there were marked differences between mainstream and special schools in the way in which pupils felt that contracts were planned and used and in their overall effectiveness. Pupils from the special schools indicated a higher level of involvement in the planning process, and in contributing to the maintenance of the contract once it had been established. They also intimated that their effectiveness in segregated locations was more apparent.

The principal questions relating to planning and organisation covered the extent of involvement of pupils in the construction of the contract. Pupils from the mainstream schools were more likely to be recipients of contracts for a cumulative set of problem behaviours, whereas special school pupils, apart from those attending schools where contracts were routinely established for all pupils, tended to be given contracts as a result of a low-incidence, high-severity behaviour (e.g. fighting). Moreover, the mainstream schools tended to use contracts or agreements as reactive devices to problem behaviours; two of the special schools used them to monitor, improve and even pre-empt problematic behaviours, a strategy well-illustrated by the contrasting experiences of two pupils: 'Sometimes you get one and sometimes you don't; it's up to which teacher you get in trouble with' (D14) 'We've all got one and we all know what its for... so do the teachers' (F60). A similar, though less formalised, system obtained in the other special schools in this study.

Over a third of the pupils reported that neither they, nor their parents or carers had been involved in the planning of the contract. The special schools were more inclined to involve parents and pupils at this initial stage of the process – over 3/4 of the pupils felt that either their teachers and pupils, or teachers, pupils and parents, had participated in the planning stage. Compared with this level of involvement the mainstream schools appeared to be less willing, or have less experience of, involving parents and pupils.

A further difference between special and mainstream schools is apparent when the content of the contract is considered. Over a quarter of pupils felt that the latter constructed contracts which sought compliance to five or more 'rules'. The special schools were more focused, with almost half their pupils reporting the use of contracts which highlighted just one or two specific behavioural requirements.

Information from the pupils indicates that, in many cases, their perception of the term 'contract' was that it was very much a one-sided agreement. Half the pupils in the sample said that neither their teachers nor parents/carers were required to make an explicit undertaking or perform a particular duty associated with the contract. The composite data shows a surprising number of 'don't know' returns concerning the role of teachers; also apparent is that more emphasis is placed, within the contract, on the role of parents/carers than on that of teachers. A larger number of pupils in special schools felt that their teachers were more involved in the working of the contract because they were required to fulfil certain requirements or duties which were written into the contract.

The pupils from special schools appeared to be less sensitive to the fact that more of their class- or school-mates knew that they had a behaviour contract. In part this may be explained by the routine, strategic use of contracts in two of the special schools. Equally, the perception that contracts are used less as a form of punishment in special schools may encourage pupils to be less secretive about their use.

A much higher proportion of pupils in the special schools were of the opinion that the contract, once established, was being implemented and maintained by the joint efforts of pupil, teacher and parents/carers (32%); only 5% of the mainstream pupils felt this to be the case. Both types of schools tended to identify one specific member of staff to deal with the day-to-day operation of the contract: this was more inclined to be the member of a senior management team in the secondary schools.

The special school pupils inferred that their teachers monitored the working of a contract far more closely than staff in the mainstream schools; in the latter, according to the pupils, 75% of issued contracts were not discussed more regularly than every two or three weeks, with over 40% of pupils indicating that their contracts were not reviewed or discussed for periods of over three weeks. In contrast, special school pupils reported that over 70% of contracts were discussed with their teachers on at least a weekly basis.

The pupils in this survey implied that, once the contract had been put into operation, the school was often less than helpful to them in their attempts to follow its requirements. Again there is a contrast in the views expressed by pupils from the two sectors. In the mainstream secondary schools 63% of the pupils believed that little was done by their teachers to assist them in fulfilling their contractual obligations, whereas about 56% of special school pupils thought that their teachers had made an effort to be supportive of them. A discrepancy was also noted in the extent to which parents/carers involved themselves in the working of a contract. 39% of the mainstream pupils reported that their parents had been supportive in this respect, whilst only 13% of special school pupils were of this opinion.

Whilst the differences between the two types of schools remain, it is encouraging to note that many of the pupils believed that the contract had actually helped them to work harder and behave better. It appeared that the contract worked best in improving the behaviour of pupils, with 64% of the sample responding that the strategy had been a positive influence in this area.

The pupils appeared confused about how being the recipient of a contract made them feel; a large number of pupils (22%) were unable, or unwilling, to summarise their feelings. An even larger number (29%) viewed contracts as a form of punishment, the mainstream secondary pupils forming the largest proportion of this group of respondents. Less than 10% of pupils expressed feelings of remorse or apology on account of the contract. Some pupils, exclusively in the special schools, said that the contract itself made them feel 'special'.

The remainder of this sub-section focuses upon the words of the pupils themselves, comprising their transcribed, *verbatim* comments concerning aspects of the effectiveness of behaviour contracts. Many of the issues identified in the questionnaire are articulated in the pupils' own words. In addition, some use has been made of the verbal and written observations of their teachers. In using this data as a means of assessing the effectiveness of contracts I will now return to some of the characteristics defined by Ayers, Clarke and Murray (*op.cit.*) as prerequisites to their use.

• *the contract must be realistic and fair*

A special school pupil noted that 'The contract has helped me a lot because it's very exact. You can't mess about because it's all written down there... what you're supposed to do. .... (teacher) was dead fair and didn't take the piss' (H64). Fairness has been referred to frequently in many accounts of the perceptions and beliefs of 'problem pupils' (Garner, 1996). It figures heavily in the commentaries on behaviour contracts by the present set of pupils. Apart from the natural injustice felt by many of the pupils at being excluded from the process of planning and implementation, many believed also that the terms of contracts were decided in a piecemeal or *ad hoc* fashion, and were applied in a non-uniform manner, according to which pupil was the recipient. A typically revealing comment, by a mainstream pupil, was that 'I don't think it has been planned enough, because some teachers don't even ask to see it' (B20), whilst another mainstream respondent argued that 'It depends on who you get to set it (the contract) up. If its .... (teacher) you know that it's going to be a piece of piss' (C31).

• *the contract must be written in language which is clear and unambiguous*

Many of the pupils interviewed felt that they did not understand the wording of their behaviour contract. One pupil pointedly admitted that he '...pretended to read it. It was too complicated' (B12). Another maintained that his contract contained '...too many big words that only they (teachers) understand' (A4). One of the issues of concern here has been that, apart from the language used in the contract, which was sometimes off-putting in its complexity, the layout and the physical appearance of the contract was unattractive. Many examples were in small typeface and comprised a whole A4 page of text, with space for the signatures at the bottom. The pupils were, understandably, dismissive of such contracts: 'Look at this... it embarrasses me. It's like a will or something that only a lawyer would understand' (D36).

- *the contract must involve pupils, parents and teachers in its construction*

Evidence from the pupils indicated that this equable arrangement was not always the case. This was particularly so in the mainstream secondary schools, where the pupil responses indicate a feeling of resentment at their non-inclusion in the process. Thus, one mainstream pupil commented that 'You don't have a say about it. You're just given the agreement and told to sign it' (B16), whilst another, referring to the lack of parental involvement, maintained that 'They make your parents come up to school and sign it' (C28). The latter situation is, perhaps, a product of the belief expressed by some of the teachers in the mainstream schools that they would not receive support from parents anyway; one teacher stated bluntly that 'The trouble is you get very little support from the parents'. Elsewhere amongst the mainstream pupils' responses there was confirmation of a top-down approach in the planning and implementation of contracts, summarised by the remark that 'Lots (of teachers) just wave it in front of you and tell you to sign it' (A8).

Nevertheless, both sets of pupils provided some significant indications that the kind of good practice recommended by Fletcher and Presland (1990) was being followed although, as indicated elsewhere in this paper, those pupils in special schools were more inclined to acknowledge these positive aspects in their comments. Illustrative of the way in which some schools attempt to foster pupil and parent involvement are the following comments: 'In our class we spent a lot of lessons in groups making up designs for the agreement and deciding what to put in it' (H59); 'We are allowed to decide what sort of contract we should have' (G45); 'The contract is good because it shows what my teachers are expected to do' C17).

Discussion

This small-scale study raises some important questions about a range of issues other than simply the efficacy of behaviour contracts. It is apparent that there is a sharp difference between those schools who have enshrined contracts within the overall behavioural ethos of the school: these schools tend to be special, rather than mainstream, schools. As one mainstream teacher stated, 'Contracts only work if the school has an agreed policy' (B11).

Moreover, the relationships established between pupils and teachers in special schools allow contracts to be more easily personalised as 'agreements' between a teacher and pupil who have arrived at some kind of equilibrium in the way they interact: this is usually based upon mutual respect, as illustrated by one pupil who remarked that 'Mr .... is in charge of the contract. I like him so I try to keep to it' (E26). This kind of arrangement is perhaps easier to sustain in smaller schools. Even there it is apparent that schools do need to be selective about (a) who is given a contract and/or (b) the precise nature and content of the contract. One special school teacher summarised this state of affairs as follows: 'I'd say that you need to be selective about who you use them with; we have to differentiate, because they are not universally applicable'.

It is also clear that there are difficulties because, according to one special school teacher: 'Establishing the agreement is straightforward, but maintaining it is not – from both the pupil's and the teachers' perspectives'. Many of the comments from pupils reveal that they are intuitively aware of the ongoing problems of keeping their contracts under review: 'Mr .... (deputy headteacher) is always stressed. He starts by saying that they'll make me stick to it (the contract), but they never do. There's always other things' (D40). Failure to apply the terms of a contract consistently, and over a period of time, is likely to be a major reason for their eventual ineffectiveness, for, as one mainstream pupil astutely observed, 'You do what's written for the first few days, but they soon forget when they see you behaving' (B15).

The differences between special schools and mainstream schools have important staff development implications. This small-scale study shows that those working in the segregated sector have much to offer their mainstream counterparts in the way that 'problem pupils' are managed. This is particular, so in respect of the support systems that the pupils felt were in place in the special schools to help them keep to the terms of their contract. These included timetabled one-to-one meetings with teachers, group discussion on a contractual issue, intervention strategies based on social skills training, and on timetabled review meetings and school-home meetings. As one special school teacher put it, 'There's little point in making an agreement and then leaving the child to his own devices'.

Finally, those contracts which have been constructed, in the pupils' opinion, as a form of punishment or as a means of supporting teachers rather than pupils, are unlikely to be successful. In the case of the former, the pupils viewed contracts in much the same way as many other forms of punishment: 'We get put on report a lot. It doesn't work at all, because we treat it like a competition' (A7) and 'Teachers are stupid if they think a bit of paper will make me behave' (D30) are typical dismissive comments on contracts. The pupils are similarly aware that some teachers use contracts as a device to secure control rather than to ameliorate inappropriate behaviour. One pupil, displaying a high degree of cynicism, believed that 'They just want evidence that you've done wrong so that's why they do it' (A2).

This chapter has sought to highlight the importance of critical reflection by whole schools on the procedures and practices it adopts when working with pupils with problems. The evidence suggests that, taking just one approach which is currently popular, namely the use of behaviour contracts, attention needs to be given not only to the way in which contracts are conceptualised, planned and implemented, but also to the belief systems of both teachers and pupils. The former requires professional development activity, in which staff from special schools can play a positive role; the latter demands a more critical look at the ethos of individual schools, and in particular the relationships between pupils and teachers. Furthermore, it may be even more relevant to suggest that the kinds of self-assessment and critical self-analysis (both organisational and individual) it points to may only materialise in schools which have accepted a view of themselves as fluid structures in which a wide range of participants, not least pupils with problems, have something to offer the commonweal. In generating this self-image a premium needs to be placed on whole-school approaches.

Chapter 5

Separate provision
a case of new wine in old bottles?

Provision for those young people who exhibit 'problem behaviour' has an unhappy tradition of inadequate funding, betraying its low-status within the education hierarchy. In spite of recent, much-heralded initiatives aimed (at least in terms of its rhetoric) at improving the educational opportunities of young people defined as having these 'problems' there is an underlying feeling of *deja-vu*, and a suggestion that these attempts merely replicate the unsatisfactory and discriminatory practices attempted in the recent past.

It is not my intention here to trace the history of segregated provision, nor to support or defend the principles (or prejudices?) which inform it. Both have been exhaustively treated elsewhere – most recently in Jenkinson (1997). Nor do I wish to carry a torch for inclusion – as others have done this elsewhere (Thomas *et al.*, 1998). What I wish to avoid is further fuel for the integration/inclusion versus segregation debate. This controversy has rumbled on since the Warnock Committee (1978), with its protagonists occasionally popping their heads above the parapet to fire at committed, but ideologically distant, colleagues working in other settings; little of that debate, it appears, incorporated the pupil with problems into an integrationist vision. What I want to do here is to consider just one aspect of segregation, the pupil referral unit (PRU), together with its recent ancestor, the quaint yet revealingly titled 'disruptive unit'. This exercise provides, firstly, an indication of the ambivalence which pervades the inclusion discussion as soon as 'pupils with problems' enter the equation. Secondly, it shows the shameful manner in which policy-makers legislate to underfund a growing population who are being excluded from mainstream provision.

The gathering pace of the inclusive education lobby has seen the focus deflected from the role of special schools and units. This shift in orientation may partly be understood in terms of an egalitarian view of social and educational justice. All children, irrespective of their disability, should have the right to participate to the full in the regular processes of society. But there appears to be a high degree of selectivity as to which children and young people are deemed to be appropriate participants. Thus, whilst it undoubtedly provides an inspiring commentary on 'the making of an inclusive school', Thomas *et al*'s study (*op.cit.*, 1998) would definitely have struck a more powerful blow had it described the closure of an EBD special school and the inclusion of its children and teachers within a mainstream setting. Thus, whilst not denying the validity of the exercise, there is scarcely a doubt that the initiative does little for the cause of the EBD population, demonstrating that inclusion for all is still a long way off.

The so-called 'disruptive units', which flourished during the 1970s and early 1980s, were the precursors of PRUs. In fact, the similarities between the two are very close, and a feeling prevails that neither has done much to advance the educational or social cause of those who are excluded from mainstream schools. Evidence to support this view has been gathered from children and teachers who have either attended or worked in 'disruptive units' or who are currently doing so in PRUs and this forms the substance of this chapter. Account is taken of the views of these two groups of informants in respect of four important issues surrounding these types of segregated provision: resourcing and accommodation, referral and reintegration policies, the curriculum and the status of both pupils and their teachers in relation to mainstream provision.

Disruptive Units and Pupil Referral Units: an historical synopsis

In the 1970s a 'new' category of child, who was termed 'disruptive', was created. This was accompanied by the establishment of extensive provision, usually in the form of euphemistically termed 'support-centres' or 'sanctuaries', which functioned as units separated from mainstream schools; such units became known in educational folklore as 'disruptive units'. Lloyd-Smith (1984) pointed out that 'The evolution of this policy, whilst being unsystematic, was both widespread and rapid, and by the end of the decade special units had become a commonplace feature of provision in most local education authorities' (p.1). The growth in provision was apparent at a time of increasing public and professional concern, in part generated by the so-called Great Debate about educational standards and particularly about discipline in schools (Lovey, Docking and Evans, 1993).

The characteristics of the kinds of facilities and opportunities, and the individual LEA policies which underpinned them, made available to 'disruptive pupils' during this time suggested a piecemeal and random pattern which verged on the eccentric (Lovey, Docking and Evans, *op.cit.*). Fuller accounts of the structure and educational arrangements of 'units' reveal that such provision often took the form of dumping grounds for difficult pupils (Mortimore, Davies, Varlaam and West, 1983). This situation was inclined to allow mainstream schools the opportunity to avoid responsibility for the problematic behaviour of some of their pupils. Moreover, it has been suggested that the institutionalisation of this group of young people has been a major contribution to their creation in the first place (Coulby, 1984).

What followed, in the 1970s and the early part of the1980s, was the operation of a large number of segregated units which, according to both contemporary and more recent analysis, was largely inadequate and inequitable (Basini, 1981: Drew, 1990). Characteristically the 'off-site unit' for disruptive pupils often comprised poorly maintained accommodation (Dempster, 1989), largely informal modes of referral (Bash, Coulby and Jones, 1985), restricted and poorly resourced curricular opportunities (Garner, 1987), and frequently inexperienced, if well-meaning, teachers (DES, 1989).

The 'son of the sanctuary' arrived with the publication of the government circulars collectively entitled 'Pupils with Problems' (DfE, 1994a-1994e). These included Circular 11/94, which was largely devoted to the education of young people in pupil referral units (PRUs). The Circular recognised that units which had previously dealt with young people who had been excluded from school 'have until now had a dubious legal status'. Moreover, it confirmed the haphazard manner of referral, stating that the 'How and why pupils are referred to units currently varies between LEAs, and between units and rarely seems to be determined by clear and consistent LEA policy' (para. 28). Accordingly, the Circular sought to promote the establishment of 'a new type of school (*sic*), to be known as a pupil referral unit' (para. 25). The Circular also indicated that existing off-site units will be henceforth termed PRUs. As in the case of off-site units in the 1970s, there are arguments which suggest that this response to 'disruptive' pupils was prompted more by the desire to state a control-policy, predicated by the views of Right-Wing 'law and order' ideologues. This movement continues unabated in spite of the failure of central government policy in many areas of health, social care and education. In a recent attack on the teaching profession, for example, Marsland (1995) called upon teachers to strengthen their pedagogical skills, particularly their ability to generate order and discipline amongst young people.

In a similar vein, the exclusion of 'problem pupils' from the mainstream and their placement in PRUs has had as much to do with the fact that this course of action would benefit other ('non-disruptive') pupils in schools. Circular 11/94 is fairly explicit in this respect, implying that it is the behaviour of such pupils which 'poses difficulties for schools', the inference being that the 'difficulties' will go away once the pupils are removed. Notwithstanding this interpretation, there can be little doubt that establishing the legal status of this category of pupils may at least serve to ensure that their education can at least be standardised and (maybe) its quality enhanced.

The position of disruptive students in PRUs as being, in essence, in receipt of non-inclusive education remained worrying. This was a major issue of criticism in the case of off-site units. Circular 11/94 blandly asserts that their aim should be 'to secure an early return to mainstream' (p.3). Evidence so far suggests that such good intentions are seldom brought to fruition, as subsequent pupil and teacher accounts from PRUs, described in the following section of the chapter, will illustrate.

Disruptive units: tales from the trenches

This part of the chapter uses historical accounts from both groups in order to provide evidence that what was provided during the 1970s and early 1980s satisfied neither the needs of the pupils termed disruptive, nor the professional interests of their teachers. Much of the material has been reported elsewhere (see Garner, 1996). The accounts gathered provide stark witness to the increasing incongruity of providing a segregated schooling at a time when the philosophy for special education was in the process of establishing the principle and practices of integration. This section will typify the drawbacks of off-site provision in each of the four crucial areas outlined in the introduction: resourcing and accommodation, referral and reintegration policies, the curriculum and the status of both pupils and their teachers in relation to mainstream provision. Interestingly, too, it provides further evidence of the gap which was apparent even then between the rhetoric of central and local government policy and the reality of those 'workers' (teachers and children) who participated in these endeavours. It is also a damning indictment of those who have become so enchanted by the rhetoric of inclusive education spin-doctors that they are in danger of failing to recognise the current selectivity of the process.

The data for this section was obtained between 1981 and 1984, when the author was working as a teacher in an off-site unit in central London (Garner, 1987). Seven students and three teachers provided their views. These are identified by the suffixes OSS 1-7 (the students) and OST 1-3 (the teachers). Individual students were interviewed, using an informal discussion format incorporating three questions: (a) why were you sent here? (b) what is the worst sort of behaviour from a boy or girl in school? and (c) what type of school do you like best? These questions were used as 'foci' around which a series of related matters could be explored, with the likelihood that the young person's responses would reveal their beliefs about their current (off-site) experience. This 'neutral' strategy was utilised because direct questioning about particular characteristics may, conversely, have prompted single-word answers, or, at worst, comments designed to meet the needs of the interviewer rather than represent the real views of the young persons involved. Comments have also been included from several teacher-colleagues, these having been extracted from a diary which the author maintained during the same period. These are the views of young people and their teachers regarding their off-site experience in four areas. Each includes a synopsis of the views expressed and exemplars highlighting particular opinions:

(a) Resourcing and accommodation

The poor level of resourcing and the often woefully inadequate accommodation housing off-site units in the 1970s and early 1980s have rapidly entered educational folklore. They have been officially recognised as being 'barren and uninviting' or, worse still, 'in serious disrepair' (DES, 1989). One student crisply summarised a situation which was common to many units: 'This place should be pulled down' (OSS 6), a view echoed by one of the teachers, who commented that 'I sometimes feel for the kids, especially in the winter and it's cold and the roof is leaking' (OST 3).

The unsatisfactory nature of off-site accommodation was referred to frequently during conversations with the students and their teachers. Often these establishments occupied redundant schools which were in a poor state of repair and in parts of inner-cities which could best be termed disadvantaged, with often high levels of property-related crime: 'Everything is falling to bits and people just make it worse with the vandalism and things' (OSS 5). Several, particularly in their natural habitat of metropolitan inner-city locations, were housed in ordinary terraced houses which remained unmodernised and, generally speaking, unsuitable for educational purposes. Little money was forthcoming from either central or local government for the refurbishment of the units, a state of affairs recognised by the teachers and students: 'We could do with some proper investment in the fabric of the place' (OST 1), The students' attitude to the buildings was frequently uncaring: 'If it was a nicer place I think I'd respect it a lot more' (OSS 4).

There was, at the time, little understanding (in the case of excluded children at least) of the principle that funds should follow pupils. Curriculum resources, for example, were largely obtained by individual and ad hoc agreements between the unit and its feeder schools ('We had some discussion about a formal capitation allowance; in the main we survive on handouts OST 1). This left huge gaps in facilities, with both students and teachers having to make do with resources which were significantly less abundant or varied than their mainstream counterparts. This state of affairs was consistently referred to by the students, as the following comments suggest: 'We never get decent stuff like computers; they give us rubbish all the time' (OSS 1); 'We've got a library here, which is a joke name. The books are too old and I'm ashamed to read them' (OSS1) and ' We have a woodwork lesson – but that's the wrong name for it because they always make excuses not to let you work with good stuff (wood)' (OSS 3).

(b) Referral and reintegration policies

These were often well-meaning, but remained chaotic and haphazard. There appeared to be few attempts at standardising referral and reintegration practices within individual LEAs. Often referrals were instantaneous, with a member of a senior management team contacting staff at the unit to let them know of the impending arrival of another new recruit. As one student observed, 'I was sent here by Mr ....; I think it was because I kept annoying him and he didn't like it' (OSS 6). The off-site teachers viewed the function of referral meetings with a high degree of cynicism: 'The Unit teachers do contribute to the discussion on placement, but you tend to think that the decision has already been made' (OST 3).

This situation, which was common in the 1970s and 1980s, militated against effective curriculum planning. It also had serious implications for the overall balance of the unit's intake, a matter which was inclined to cause recurrent problems because of the small size of the unit and the high degree of interpersonal contact between those working in them. The teachers in such units were often the victims of their own guilt feelings, which persuaded them to accept new referrals, however inappropriate: 'We can never say 'no' to a pupil who has been excluded; we know that the unit is the only place he's got' (OST 3).

Approaches to reintegration into the mainstream fared little better. There was a widely held belief that once a young person was referred out to an off-site unit s/he would seldom make a successful return to the school of origin: 'I came down here one day and they said this was where I was going to stay' (OSS 4). The official rhetoric has always been to the contrary, with OFSTED (1993) stating that 'Effective schools pay careful attention to the re-entry of any excluded children'. Both students and staff from the off-site units used in this chapter were not optimistic of the chances of reintegration. 'They had a meeting and said I was out; I had to come to the sanctuary to cool off. I've been here ever since' (OSS 7).

Both students and teachers held mixed views about a return to the mainstream. A number of students welcomed the prospect of returning to their original school: 'Sometimes I'd like to go back up there because I've got mates there' (OSS 4). But there was a widespread feeling of alienation from the mainstream from both students and teachers, a situation exemplified by such remarks as 'I go back three times a week for Art. Some of the teachers think I'm stupid' (OSS 6); 'Once I went back up with Miss .... and it only lasted half an hour; Mr .... (senior teacher) started on at me in front of some others, and I wasn't going to stand for that' (OSS

5), and 'I hate going up to …. (mainstream school) with one of the boys. I feel really threatened and on edge' (OST 1).

(c) The Curriculum

The generally inadequate levels of resourcing experienced by off-site units resulted in curriculum provision which often fell a long way short of the 'broad, balanced, relevant and differentiated' approach recommended by HM government over ten years ago (DES, 1985). A typical reference to this state of affairs, by one off-site student, was that 'We don't get much variety; always Maths and English every morning (OSS 2), supported by another's view that 'None of us can do the things we're good at because there's no facilities – like MVS (motor vehicle studies)' (OSS 5).

In part this situation arose because of the small size of most off-site units. Invariably the maximum number of pupils on roll was between 24 and 36, with a staffing ratio of 1:6. Several subjects had to be covered by one teacher, and the lack of specialisation meant that some subjects (for instance Science and Technology) received only passing attention, a situation frequently noted by the teachers views that 'We do our best to give the kids here variety. But the four of us have to cover the whole curriculum, which is a tall order' (OST 2) and that 'None of us knows anything about Science – we're mainly ex-art teachers' (OST 1).

The haphazard nature of providing for curriculum materials, referred to in an earlier section, had a similar, restricting effect. The teachers participating in this study felt that the educational experience they offered to the students was generally unsatisfactory and merely served a containing role: 'It can be a bit depressing because we know that the curriculum we offer is simply just there to keep them occupied' (OST 1).

(d) Pupil and Teacher status

The 'disruptive' young people in off-site units, being assigned to a non-formal (and therefore low-status SEN), held firm beliefs about their place in the overall educational hierarchy. This was reinforced by what they saw around them: the poor state of repair of their unit, the inadequate curriculum facilities, and their perception of (some of) their teachers as little more than well-meaning social workers who lacked the status of their mainstream counterparts. Such beliefs only contributed to what, in many young people attending off-site units, was a chronically low self-esteem.

The students from the off-site units made copious reference to their mainstream school when explaining how they felt. Many expressed anger at the way in which others saw them, stating that 'When I go back up to .... (mainstream school) some of the teachers give me stick. They never let it rest' (OSS 4) and that 'They think I'm crazy just because of one or two things. Everyone is a bit mad when something bugs them' (OSS 2). It is noteworthy that several students in this study provided evidence of a degree of optimism in their own educational outcomes; this was usually associated with obtaining a place in further education: 'We're not going to get anywhere with all this. It'll be different when I get to college' (OSS1).

Their teachers, too, were inclined to identify with such negative impressions: 'I think this is just a kind of glorified child minding – it certainly wasn't what I'd trained for' (OST 2). Often they felt under-valued, a perception which was reinforced by their experience of referral/reintegration, where they considered that their viewpoint was seldom given appropriate weight in resulting decision making. The feeling, indicated by the off-site teachers' comments was that, compared with their mainstream colleagues, they were second-class citizens: 'I don't reckon I am viewed as a proper teacher by staff from and ... (mainstream schools)' (OST 3).

Marcel Proust is alive and well: views from the PRUs

Go into a typical PRU and you will encounter pretty much the same conditions as were the norm in 'disruptive units'. If Proust was a contemporary teacher he would have little difficulty in grasping the essence of what currently comprises 'off-site' practice and using it to make a journey to the past. A series of unstructured conversations were conducted with students and teachers in two PRUs in the Greater London area during the summer term, 1995. Statements from nine students (indicated by the suffix PRS 1-9) and two teachers (indicated by the suffix PRT 1 or 2) provide the data in this section. The conversation strategy with the students replicated the approach used approximately ten years previously in the off-site unit. A further set of comments were elicited from teachers in both PRUs. Both made use of the original three questions, as used in the off-site unit conversations, the intention being to ascertain participants' views in the same four areas of concern as noted earlier for the off-site units. The views of both the young people and their teachers are again briefly summarised.

(a) Resourcing and accommodation

Some LEAs, using central government funds, have been able to provide levels of resourcing and accommodation which outstrip those in the earlier offsite units: 'The LEA spent quite a bit of money making repairs and generally refurbishing prior to our opening' (PRT1). The two PRUs represented in this study, however, replicated the unsatisfactory accommodation of their off-site predecessors, with one student scathingly recognising that 'This place got a new sign outside, but its still the same old dump it used to be last year' (PRS 2).

The PRUs involved in the study were sited in redundant primary or special schools ('This place could be better. It's like a primary school really' PRS 4). The location of the PRUs, replicating that of the off-site units, led to continued difficulties, with one teacher noting that 'We suffer a lot because of vandalism to the premises out of school hours' (PRT 2).

Both young people and teachers felt that the inadequacies of the building led to unnecessary tensions between them, suggested in one student's comments that 'They said they'd give us proper equipment and things that were interesting. It was stupid to think things would be different'(PRS 6) and that 'nothing works properly and they (the teachers) say we've got to be patient all the time' (PRS 6).

An additional difficulty was that the expectations of the young people to have access to more sophisticated curriculum materials (including computers, CDROM and technology resources) were significantly greater than their off-site counterparts in the 1970s and 1980s. Thus, two of the students indicated that 'My mates have got better computers at home than what we've got here' (PRS 7) and that 'We are expected to work with equipment that is years old. It should all be dumped' (PRS 9). The lack of appropriate resources in PRUs suggests deleterious effect on the self-image of the students (and the teachers), one member of staff observing that 'We could do with more substantial allowances to obtain curriculum materials and resources so that our students don't feel like second-class citizens' (PRT 1).

(b) Referral and reintegration policies

There was some cause for optimism expressed by both young people and their teachers in the PRUs. The excluded youngsters at least felt that they knew the real reason for their placement in the unit 'I'm here because I just couldn't get on in that place (mainstream school, and especially because I had rows all the time with Mr .... (PRS 4), and generally felt positive towards their new situation ('I'm comfortable here and don't want to go back to .... mainstream school (PRS 3).

Nonetheless there was a generally held belief that they would now complete their education in a PRU, with few students holding out much hope for a strategic return to the mainstream. One student, for example, said that he would 'like to go back up to (mainstream school) but they always find an excuse not to have me back there' (PRS 2). Nor were the students complimentary about their own role in the referral/reintegration procedure. They felt, as did their off-site counterparts before them, that their views were seldom taken into account. The comments of two students clearly illustrate this: 'In this (review) meeting they asked me what I felt. I said they were bastards and I got kicked out; they didn't ask me why I said it' (PRS 1) and 'I never got a say. Mr (Head of Year) was all right, but everyone knew I'd end up here' (PRS 8).

The PRU teachers were in the main dismissive and cynical of the concept of reintegration. Their view was that late referral to PRUs (the average age of referrals in the two units was 14.7 years) meant that the pupils involved had experienced several years of unsatisfactory provision in their mainstream school and were generally unwilling to return. The teachers consequently adopted a pragmatic standpoint, one stating that 'Most of the staff here are realists. The kids we deal with don't stand a cat in hell's chance of returning to mainstream' (PRT 1).

Moreover, the same cynicism concerning referral and reintegration, originally manifest by teachers in the off-site units, was replicated by those working in the PRUs. The teachers felt that their views, like those of their students, were frequently overlooked and that issues relating to placement were 'like battles of will – it's us against the school and the LEA ' (PRT 1) in which 'We are in a no-win situation;the Authority pays our wages and we have to toe the line on things like admissions' (PRT 2).

(c) The curriculum

The curriculum arrangements of PRUs, whilst showing some evidence of breadth and balance, were nevertheless more restricted than the mainstream equivalent. This was a feature of the PRUs that many of the young people saw as problematic: 'It's OK, but I get sick of having .... (teachers name) for nearly every lesson. It gets boring' (PRS 5) and 'We don't get the same variety as up at .... (mainstream school); the stuff we do just keeps us occupied' (PRS 7) typify this feeling.

Some focused in particular upon the restricted series of options open to them in examinable subjects, although there was evidence that few of these young people considered public examination success as being relevant to them in the long run: 'I'm supposed to be doing 3 GCSEs, but I don't think I stand much chance. I'll do all right without them I suppose' (PRS 2). One student complained that, whilst he was following a GCSE course in Geography he 'wasn't allowed to go on the field trip' (PRS 3), which was an essential for final assessment.

The teachers in the two PRUs felt that, with more frequent liaison with their colleagues in mainstream schools, they could provide a more effective curriculum. Thus, one teacher felt that 'Some of these kids would easily be able to pass GCSEs, providing they were given the opportunity: that requires a lot more cooperation with the mainstream schools, which we don't get.' (PRT 2). The teachers pointed in particular to the difficulties of arranging meetings with subject-teachers in mainstream schools, and felt that the ensuring young people in PRUs kept abreast with their subject studies once they were placed off-site was virtually insurmountable, stating that 'As a staff group we often feel frustrated that we cannot offer the breadth of experiences that they would get in a mainstream situation'(PRT 1).

(d) Pupil and Teacher status

Both young people and their teachers in the PRUs showed that they believed themselves to be inferior to their respective mainstream counterparts. The young people in the PRUs felt that many of their mainstream peers looked down on them 'You can tell that most of the teachers don't respect you' (PRS 5); They talk to you different and never let you have an opinion' (PRS 9), and regarded them as 'unbalanced' or 'out of order' PRS 4). 'They just thought I was a nutter, stupid...'; PRS 4) They had little contact with their peers in ordinary schools, and resisted moves towards their reintegration apart from those few subjects taught by teachers they felt they could trust.

The teachers seemed to hold ambivalent views about their professional status. On the one hand there was evidence of considerable commitment to this group of youngsters ('I work here because I think I can do something to change things'; PRT 1) matched by an understanding of the socio-political connotations of the work they were doing ('I get sick of all the hypocrisy about these places: they are sink-schools, a last resort and everybody knows it'; PRT 1). But these teachers were also highly cynical of both public and professional attitudes to them and those they taught. This cynicism was directed particularly at a number of unsupportive mainstream colleagues encountered in referral or review meetings. One teacher expressed this feeling in a very direct way, stating that 'I think teachers working in mainstream should spend a couple of days a year down here. They are the ones who cause a lot of the difficulties anyway' (PRT 2).

No new wine... only old bottles

The accounts presented in this chapter, drawn from both students and their teachers, suggest that little has changed in the lot of those who are 'on the margins' (Lloyd-Smith and Davies, 1996) of the normative educational provision in English schools. Whilst the evidence presented is largely anecdotal, it does little to detract from a prevailing view that the most recent 'innovations' for those who have been excluded comprise protocols and bureaucratic procedures. Little, it appears, has been forthcoming to enable 'problem pupils' to return to the educational system that, to a large extent, has been instrumental in ostracising them; and it remains to be seen whether the formulation of LEA Behaviour Support Plans, as required by section 9 of the 1997 Education Act, will provide cause for a dramatic reevaluation of this situation.

PRUs are required to function in a political climate in which the dominant educational ideology has shifted towards a market orientation. The effects of the 1988 Education Act in particular, in which schools were given the choice to opt out of local authority control, have done much to promote a situation in which

> young people with special educational needs or difficult behaviour may not be seen as contributing positively to the performance of the school. Headteachers and governors may become less tolerant and more likely to exclude pupils presenting difficult behaviour from mainstream education (The Childrens Society, 1993)

There are also signs of a hardening attitude on the part of individual teachers towards students who misbehave (Bush and Hill, 1993). One depressing indication of this is the extent to which 'assertive discipline' (Canter, 1982), which assumes that if a student breaks a school rule (s)he must pay the consequences. The sanctions imposed, often comprising public reprimands, do little to enhance the already shattered self-esteem of many problem students.

Furthermore PRUs, whilst being required to satisfy the requirements of the 1993 Education Act with regard to a balanced and broadly based curriculum, 'are not bound to provide the full National Curriculum' (DfE,1994). Nor are they required to 'conduct statutory assessments of students at or near to the end of each Key Stage' (DfE, 1994). Students within PRUs are therefore placed in a situation which has historical parallels in off-site units. Both groups of students have had little assistance from the legislator in securing curricular entitlement.

Fifteen years of so-called development, applying the collective wisdom of the great and the good, has merely served to emphasise that 'disruptive' or problem pupils will always be seen as a threat, to be controlled either by overtly punitive regimes (like the Tory suggestion for the creation of the equivalent of US-style boot camps) or by platitudes and rhetoric, with little in the way of appropriate funding levels to secure more meaningful and long-term solutions to what, by any reasonable logic, should not be an intractable problem. Nor is there evidence of serious attempts by administrators, legislators and politicians to listen to what this group of young people have to say about the education system, in spite of growing evidence that such approaches can have beneficial effects on schools and individuals (Schools Councils U.K., 1994). Elsewhere there are ominous signs that the uncertain future for 'pupils with problems' may become even more tenuous, as they become a pawn in power struggles between teacher-unions and central government. Official and professional thinking continues to be locked in a time warp, the DfEE having successfully bottled the 'off-site formula' so that it may be sniffed again in Proustian vein. *Plus ca change, plus ce meme chose.*

Chapter 6

Can the curriculum make a difference?

Introduction

Over fifty years ago the School Health regulations of 1945, in defining the term 'maladjusted pupils', stated that these were children who '...require special educational treatment in order to effect their personal, social or educational readjustment'. Such 'readjustment', according to Laslett (1990), is unlikely to be achieved by '... teaching the same subjects as the ordinary school rather differently with different teachers'.

More recently, Marchant (1995) has argued that '...the essential core curriculum for pupils experiencing emotional and behavioural difficulties (EBD) is the expression of their own feelings and emotions to facilitate greater control over their own lives' (p.46). He goes on to state that 'The provision of a formal, academic, curriculum is of only secondary importance....'. An official recognition of this aspect of social learning is contained in the inspection framework for schools (OFSTED, 1995), in which inspectors have to indicate the degree to which a school is promoting self-discipline and the development of self-esteem.

In spite of this there is considerable tension between what O'Brien (1998) has described as the 'competing ideologies' of healing or learning. He argues that 'Children with emotional and behavioural difficulties can gain the therapeutic benefits of emotional 'recovery and development' by raising their self-esteem through achievement and attainment in the whole curriculum, which includes the National Curriculum' (p.32). Elsewhere, in drawing from a particular EBD school's policy statement, it is stated that 'In an EBD school the children should receive the National Curriculum. The remaining curriculum time might be focused on their distinct and particular social and emotional needs' (p.27). The two statements appear to me to be contradictory, even fatuous. As I argue in this chapter, using the example of a small group of pupils in PRUs, there is an illogicality in a special setting providing 'more of the same' (Daniels, 1990) in terms of curriculum; by all means maximise the opportunities for these youngsters to receive high-quality (National) curriculum input – but do not allow a slavish pursuance of dogma to deflect from a consideration of the very issue that brought the pupil to the special setting in the first place, namely his (sic) inappropriate behaviour, betraying, amongst other things, a lack of social skills.

Once again, the chapter utilises the evidence provided by the key actors in what has become a long-running soap opera; these are those individuals whose opinions have largely been ignored – unlike the Ken Barlows of 'real life' versions, for whom a hungry media provides a platform for off-loading all sorts of unctuous or vindictive opinion. Ultimately the pupils themselves illustrate the nature, extent and relevance of a 'social curriculum' and its influence on the future social inclusion of 'pupils with problems'.

In moving along this pathway, however, I am not advocating a marginalisation of the formal, taught National Curriculum. Indeed, I am somewhat closer to O'Brien's sentiments than my previous remarks suggest. Thus, I totally empathise with the view, neatly characterised by the exhortation that 'EBD schools should aim to demonstrate the features of an effective school' (O'Brien, op.cit.). What I am seeking to explore here is the precise nature of that effectiveness, particularly in respect of the specified needs of the pupils themselves. It is my belief, by no means new or radical, that the National Curriculum can be made an integral part of a more holistic, social curriculum – rather than the other way around.

In support of this assertion the chapter explores a possible reality gap which exists between the official version, as exemplified by various statutory or guidance documents, and the formal, social curriculum experienced by students in PRUs. Thus, in spite of official claims that schools, '...when planning the curriculum for pupils with special educational needs... (should include)... the recognition, within the wider curriculum, of the importance of specific aspects of work, such as personal, social and health education' (SCAA, 1996, p.9), the demands of the academic curriculum have resulted in a noticeable diminution in the amount of time devoted to this aspect of work in schools, and, in this case, PRUs.

A rationale for a personal and social skills focus within the curriculum is mapped in the first section of the chapter. The extent to which the principles and practices in this overview form a significant part of the operational reality of PRUs is then examined, using some examples taken from the transcripts of an initial set of interviews with pupils and their teachers. Comparison is also made between the curricular experiences of pupils deemed to be 'at risk' of exclusion by teachers whilst still placed in mainstream settings. This dual focus allows two practical issues to be explored: to what extent are the emotional and/or behavioural needs of pupils being met by mainstream schools? And, if they are unsatisfactorily met in such locations – with the likely outcome being exclusion – do PRUs address these pupil-needs in a more relevant way?

The pastoral imperative

Lang (1990) has provided a general validation of the significance of pastoral care programmes in the context of a whole curriculum, arguing that '...through such provision and the resulting promotion of positive school climate and ethos, not only will the healthy personal development of all pupils be encouraged but problems of pupil disaffection and disruption ameliorated' (pp.94-95). SCAA (1996) seems to accept this view, stating that pupils with SEN '...may require additional, possibly specialist activities, to support their development, such as: aspects of personal, social and health education, including independence and study skills' (p.6). Teachers working in segregated settings, too, provide a *real politique* justification, regarding social and life-skills programmes as a fundamental way of meeting the needs of this marginalised group of SEN pupils.

Both philosophical and pragmatic justification for adopting an alternative version of curriculum provision for 'pupils with problems', which emphasises the 'social' within the curriculum, has been a common feature of the history of special education. What all of these versions of schooling have in common is a belief that a child's emotions, his responses to what is around him, and his interactions with others, are precisely the things whose dysfunction resulted in him being identified as having 'a problem'.

Goffman (1959) talked about the 'situated self', in which individuals are seen not simply in terms of personality or intellectual functioning, but as beings who identify self-implicit understandings in everything that happens to them. Pastoral care, and the domain of the 'social' in school curricula, is fundamentally concerned with the task of developing self-actualisation. Most children are supported by sets of values which have been internalised and understood in a manner which Siegel (1982) has described as '...an ability to consider consistently and without contradiction the interests and intentions of others: to act bearing these in mind and without the guidance of a superior authority and to generalise this behaviour in all relevant situations' (p.2).

One of the most important validations of a curriculum approach which focused upon the emotions and feelings was provided by Edgecumbe (1977). Her interest lay particularly in the boundary which exists between education and therapy. The former, according to Edgecumbe, '...is the contribution made by the child's teachers to his development, especially in the areas of learning and socialisation' and seeks '...to aid the growth of independence... and the establishment of a wide variety of mature relationships via enjoyment of interaction and cooperation with peers and teachers' (p.2). Therapy, on the other hand, '...is primarily intended for the treatment of a specific type of disturbance' and '...directs the child's attention inwards, to the exploration of his internal psychic condition' (p.2).

The two orientations are explicitly encountered in Steiner's (1910) philosophy that the nature of Man comprises body, soul and spirit. Each interacts with the other, either in a known, or, more frequently, in an unknown, manner. What Steiner, and subsequently those who adopted his unique philosophy, have affirmed is that, because of this interaction, education and therapy are also inseparable. Extending this argument still further, there is a version which suggests that the academic and pastoral components of the curriculum, particularly for the 'pupil with problems', are mutually dependent.

Regrettably, during the last 20 years, little approbation has been directed towards curriculum approaches which focus on the child, rather than upon the subject. There has been a preoccupation, particularly since the 1988 Education Act, with subject knowledge and outcomes. The heritage of child-centredness, from which a pastoral curriculum has grown, has been brutally dispensed with: Montessori, Pestalozzi and the Plowden advocates have been indicted because their interpretation of curriculum began with exploration of self, the feelings and emotions. As Darling (1994) commented 'Child-centred teaching finally fell from official grace in 1992. Just as approval had been indicated through the Plowden Report twenty-five years earlier, ignominy and banishment were signalled by three educationists who had been hand-picked by the DES' ... (they) dismissed discovery learning ... (and) recommended more subject-based lessons' (p.108). These new arrangements would ensure that little room would be available for the pastoral aspects of the curriculum.

The skills and experiences which pupils need as social beings cannot simply be taught as a 'body of knowledge'. Lovey, Docking and Evans (1993), for example, reported in their research that '...many teachers maintained that their most important contribution to PSE (Personal and Social Education) was informal interaction with pupils and in providing a positive atmosphere rather than in organising structured timetabled work' (p.46). Similarly, they suggest that counselling 'pupils with problems', itself an important component of a pastoral curriculum, is most effective when it is carried out informally. In this sense, therefore, content and pedagogy are inextricably linked. This may be a major factor in justifying curriculum intervention of this nature, particularly in an educational environment which is currently predicated by competencies and measured outcomes. A further point at issue is the so-called pastoral-academic divide, which has been so apparent in many secondary schools. This separation, according to Smith (1996), has deleterious effects on children who have learning difficulties, a group which has close correspondence with 'pupils with problems'.

Schools do not begin this process on an empty canvas. Hoghughi (1983) has observed, 'The child, by the time he comes to school, is not a clean slate... As a result of his treatment by his parents he has developed, to varying levels, some survival skills, social habits and ways of coping with other people' (p.127). Further development of these skills is an important function of a school's pastoral curriculum, and as a means of promoting future social self-actualisation and adjustment.

In much the same way that Karl Konig (1959) believed that 'Modern psychology has the greatest difficulty in discovering the reality of the living soul', so too can it be said that curriculum planners and legislators have displayed a level of intransigence and humbug in the way that they have consistently denied the importance of what Konig himself would perhaps have regarded as the soul of the curriculum. A tour of the recent history of curriculum developments for pupils whose behaviour in schools is deemed unsatisfactory is illustrative of this bankrupt belief system, as recent official critiques themselves have indicated (OFSTED, 1996).

Taking it to the people

The excerpts below are drawn from two sets of data, both of which explore the opinions of 'pupils with problems' concerning the 'personal and social education' element of the curriculum. Four metropolitan LEAs were selected randomly, and from each of these one mainstream secondary school (11-16) was randomly chosen. LEAs utilised in other studies described elsewhere in this book were not considered. One PRU in each LEA was also selected – although in this instance the researcher had personal/ professional contacts in each. Headteachers of each of the four mainstream schools, together with the heads of the PRUs, were approached, requesting permission to talk with both pupils and teachers. Selection of pupil 'informants' from the mainstream settings was made by their teachers, who were asked to identify six pupils who they regarded to be at risk of exclusion because of their 'problem behaviour'. Six pupil-informants from the PRUs were selected on the basis of their roll-number in the PRU (ie. numbers 1-6 in each PRU).

Pupil comments in both locations have been obtained using an informal interview format, RDFP. In this pupils were invited to comment on four aspects of their 'personal and social education': (a) *recognising* their feelings and emotions (b) *dealing* with them on an individual level (c) *facilitating* effective social interaction and (d) *planning* for their social future. Each of these general themes had been identified in a set of interviews with six teachers who worked with 'pupils with problems' in either mainstream or special school settings. All respondents were given the opportunity to review their comments, on the understanding that anything they subsequently disagreed with would be struck from the research record if they so wished. Teacher-comment was obtained from informal conversation with staff working in each of the mainstream schools and PRUs, with the same proviso. All real names, of pupils, teachers and schools, were disguised to ensure confidentiality.

Learning to Be? Pupils' and teachers' views of Personal and Social Education

The first set of extracts refers to the views of pupils who, having been excluded from mainstream schools, are being educated in PRUs located in four metropolitan LEAs; the second group relates some of the opinions expressed by (other) pupils who have been identified as being 'at risk of exclusion' by key teachers in mainstream secondary schools in the same four metropolitan LEAs. Sets of indicative comments from the teachers involved in both settings are also included. I have included 'raw' data, with some observations of my own. Whilst recognising that much of the latter is, at this stage of the study, largely impressionistic and driven by a personal belief-system, nevertheless there is a persuasiveness about the arguments presented in the verbatim comments of the 'actors' most closely involved which allows me to shy away from attempting to justify this approach.

(i) Mainstream experiences
Pupil-comment
Recognising
'They never talked to me about what I was feeling at the time... they just tell you you're bad... that's it... end of the story' (Mainstream Pupil 1)

'Sometimes I'd be bursting with anger about stuff. I'd want to say what I was thinking about all of the shit and stuff. Nobody... apart from Sambrook (*teacher*) wanted to know about anything about me' (MP1)

'He said I'd gone over the top... and that rules were rules... I did it, and I had to be punished. He was the judge... I accepted my punishment' (MP3)

'Teachers don't give a toss about us or the way we think. They're interested in other things' (MP6)

Dealing
'Mr Garman calls us in and gives us a lecture... like he's giving out instructions in the gym. You don't take no notice of that' (MP5)

'They keep saying 'count to three before you react'... I could count to 100 and still want to kill the bastard' (MP3)

'Denning sets you targets. Some of the new kids accept it... but we just treat it like a game' (MP2)

Facilitating

'In tutor groups we're told about wars and that... and he (*form tutor*) says that it'll all be alright if we just get on with each other' (MP4)

'I hate some kids. They're always right, always picked to do good stuff. I look after me. Fuck the rest... only Jonno and me count' (MP2)

'You sit in a circle and say good things about people. You don't mean it... you just go along with it' (MP5)

Planning

'When I leave here I'm going to look after me. No-one else gives a shit, so I've got to' (MP6)

'You stand on your own... don't take crap from anyone... otherwise you're nothing' (MP1)

'My mates rob sometimes if they're short (*of money*) and... I'll rob as well if it gets me what I want' (MP2).

One inference to be drawn from the foregoing is that teachers in mainstream settings, under pressure to conform to sets of rigid expectations and performances, are unlikely to forego these responsibilities in favour of an emphasis on emotional well-being. As Peagam (1995) has remarked '...recent legislation (especially the 1988 Education Act) and official reports which influence the professional and contractual expectations laid on teachers have emphasised that the primary responsibility of teachers and schools to all children is the development of skills, knowledge and understanding' (p.13). They are also indicative of a rising level of militancy amongst teachers, well illustrated by recent events publicised in the media, which has lowered a threshold of tolerance to inappropriate or non-normative behaviours.

Pressures on time, and a perceptible diminution of 'pastoral staff' in many schools in recent years, has resulted in the ascendancy of quick-fix solutions, aimed at controlling behaviour rather than understanding it. The rule-governed ethos of schools, as the pupils' comments imply are unlikely to result in a shared approach to managing behaviour. This is an important issue; as Royer (1995) remarks '...the school must teach social competence to students who are at risk of disciplinary actions such as suspension or expulsion. In order to be validated and reinforced, and achieve the necessary social reciprocity, these skills must be chosen by the adolescent in collaboration with his peers, teachers and parents' (p.35).

Teacher-comment

'We have to teach certain things. We all know that they are completely irrelevant to the kids you're doing research about' (Mainstream Teacher 1)

'I'd turn the clock back 20 years... at least then we were giving those pupils something that meant a bit to them' (MT3)

'The National Curriculum has killed off a lot of the really useful work I was able to do with them' (MP4)

'I don't see how you can deal with all the crap out there. You talk to your tutor group... but you know they've far more experience than you' (MT6)

There is a depressing familiarity (and similarity) in the observations of mainstream teachers gathered as part of this project. There was almost universal agreement that the National Curriculum, and the onset of a 'free education market', had severely inhibited the chances of teachers in mainstream schools of adopting curriculum initiatives which might more readily address the needs of 'pupils with problems'. Certainly, their views appear to be at odds with the romanticised version of pastoral care, outlined by Courtman (1996) as being indicative of current practice, wherein it has been able to maintain an emphasis upon '...a school culture and ethos based on the quality of communication and relationships that place the need of the child at the centre of educational experience' (p.3).

(ii) PRU experiences

Recognising

'I know now why I'm here... it's because of my temper getting out of hand' (PRP2)

'I talk a lot more now (about myself)... and it's good... especially because we go over things and find out about why I done things like that' (PRP3)

'Teachers here know all about me and my reputation... but I like it because they don't sit there like some judge or copper... (and) I can see things I've done better' (PRP5)

'I used to say it wasn't me. Now I know it was definitely me... (well... some of the time) (PRP4)

Dealing

'We sit around and talk about things... the way we are and that... a lot more... it didn't happen like this at Eastwood (*school*)... we always had to be doing this or that' (PRP1)

'I work with Mrs Derrington and she gives me ideas about how not to get into trouble... I do this every day for about half an hour' (PRP3)

'We get set times to go through why I behave like I do. Sometimes it's good because I can see how stupid I've been' (PRP4)

'There's stuff planned for me like I never got at the other place. I'm not saying I agree with what (they) say about me all the time... but it helps me think in a better way' (PRP6)

Facilitating

'A lot of the time we do role-plays and we have to imagine us being someone else. That's good 'cos you can appreciate somebody's opinions more' (PRP1)

'We get rewards for helping others and rewards for keeping our tempers. I'm in Band A now and I'm going to use my tokens to go on the fun day' (PRP6)

'I still get (f...ing) angry... especially when things don't go my way. But it's a lot better than before because of the (*social skills*) lessons with Mrs Derrington (PRP3)

Planning

'They're helping me to go to college. I want to get some qualifications. I reckon I've got a good chance because I'm better at talking now' (PRP5)

'I wouldn't say I've changed much, but I'm not as bad as I was... I think it'll help me later (PRP2)

The comments of the pupils in PRUs are notable in their prevailing sense of optimism. They would certainly appear to be at odds with the most recent comments on PRU provision (OFSTED, 1996; Garner, 1996). They would reflect more accurately the (largely subjective) data presented by Fisher (1996), whose overview of curricular provision in PRUs concludes that 'it is evident that the search for an answer (to supporting pupils in difficulty) is being conducted with considerable vigour' (p.18). He reports that the emphasis on social aspects of the curriculum is being maintained, and uses a range of documentary evidence to support this assertion: indicative of this is the example of the London Borough of Lambeth, where 'The curriculum is designed to promote students' overall development and prepare them for the opportunities, responsibilities and experiences of life' (p.16).

Amidst this positive perspective, the spectre of labelling, non-inclusion and narrowness of curriculum provision is always apparent. Powerful lobby-groups, advocating an end to segregated provision on the grounds of social justice and equality, have provided an important crutch to those wishing to retain the non-provision for 'pupils with problems' which currently obtains in mainstream settings. PRUs, in this respect, are set to join a diminishing band of 'EBD' (Emotional and/or Behavioural Difficulties) schools who are fighting a rearguard action for their place as key providers of the 'social' in the curriculum – provision which, they maintain, is best suited to the holistic needs of this group of pupils.

Teacher-comment

'I was really angry with the OFSTED report on PRUs. It gave the wrong impression of us and was totally negative' (PRT2)

'I'd say we spend more time ironing out the social problems of these kids than we do on the National Curriculum' (PRT4)

'I think you can't separate the social work we do from anything else – yet they all seem to want us to concentrate on academic learning' (PRT1)

Teachers working in separate settings – in this case PRUs – seem to adopt a pragmatic, yet heavily ideological view, of the work they do. Visser, quoted recently, summarises the views of many working with 'pupils with problems': '...you might not be following the national curriculum to the letter, but you will be achieving a great deal' (TES, December 6, 1996). They are acutely aware of the intrinsic need for a level of curriculum flexibility to address those needs which underpin the very categorisation 'pupils with problems'.

So?

The data collected suggest that the imposition of a National Curriculum, with its attendant 'academic' focus and its assessment, has had a deleterious effect on the ability of mainstream schools to offer strategic, concentrated and long-term intervention for pupils who are at-risk of exclusion. As Garner and Sandow (1993) have put it:

'PSE at any level is hardly assessable in attainment target terms: one can imagine perhaps ('Level 1: can recognise the difference between own and others' property'). Frankly, there is little time in the new framework for activities which cannot be assessed. They may feature in Records of Achievement... they are clearly perceived as peripheral to 'real education' (p.26).

This is not to say that good work of a pastoral focus is not taking place in mainstream schools. But such work has to function within a theoretical framework which makes some general, though often unspoken, assumptions about this process:

- that education is a good thing.

- that if it works properly, students will not only become literate and numerate, but will grow up as 'good' citizens

- that the inclusion of subjects such as 'civics', 'citizenship' and 'life skills' in the curriculum create good citizens in adult life.

How this is currently being done in many mainstream settings is a point at issue, and needs to be seen against a background of the prevailing belief-systems about education itself. The view of school as a place where children are taught things within a clearly defined (usually hierarchical) social context by a group of suitably qualified adults has always been a simplistic one. Sociological analysis in education over the last 20 years has gradually revealed the interpersonal nature of school life, especially in the investigation of the 'hidden curriculum'. This has led, amongst other things, to a heightened awareness of the pupil's experience of schooling, and the role that this process plays in the development of attitudes and responses in later life.

Given the constraints of time in the post-1988 school curriculum, referred to earlier, it is likely that pastoral programmes in mainstream schools are more inclined to adopt a conventional, information-giving approach, where the content, pedagogy and rules are adult-determined and involve the identification of very clear instructions for daily behaviour. In addition, such an approach is often reinforced by the hidden curriculum of the school, as it is perceived by 'pupils with problems'. Often, for example, 'codes of conduct' and 'behaviour policies' are rule-governed and hierarchical, allowing no input or decision-making by pupils. Excluded from these events, the oppositional stance of some 'pupils with problems' is simply reinforced.

In spite of the negative assessment of OFSTED (1996), the work of PRUs appears to adopt a more meaningful and relevant approach to the needs of 'pupils with problems'. Of course, a major focus of worry amongst staff in PRUs is that, being classified as 'schools', they are subject to the same rigid curriculum format and inspection regimes. This may be a major factor inhibiting the development of positive alternatives which incorporate a more significant emphasis on personal and social education.

Whilst I have used the exemplar of PRUs in this chapter, the implications of some of my arguments extend far beyond them. If staff working in dedicated provision for pupils with problems feel that they have to jump through the same curriculum hoops as their counterparts in mainstream settings, there would appear to be very little chance of sustained innovation in (particularly) secondary schools which are under ever-increasing official scrutiny. Fear of failure means that risk-taking curriculum modifications are conspicuous by their absence.

So why do more of the same? In some schools a familiar comment from teachers is that 'I spend more time keeping order than teaching'. Two contributing factors create such a situation. One is most definitely rooted in what is taught and how. The National Curriculum can be an enchanted garden, providing that the needs and interests of the learner do not constantly pay second-fiddle to the career-educationists' blueprint. But even if that Holy Grail of a 'broad, balanced, relevant and differentiated' curriculum were obtained, and orchestrated by a series of (super)teachers, there would still be an underlying factor which might result in continued unwanted behaviour. Simply put, many pupils with problems are perceived as such because they do not have the appropriate interactional machinery and sense of 'self' to be able to manage themselves in particular situations. The illustrations given in this chapter, though small-scale, aptly demonstrate the need for radicalism of a kind which would recall the hey-day of the Schools Council, or the innovative practice in therapeutic schools for children with EBD. The diet of curriculum authoritarianism that has been fed to teachers over the last ten years has also promoted an easy condemnation of child-centred, problem-solving curricula and of the literature which promotes it. For all teachers, and particularly those working mainly with pupils with problems, this represents a considerable educational heritage – and it would be unheard of to demolish a Grade 1 listed building. In a society that finds it all too easy to allow systemic abuse of children, the hidden effects of this destruction of all that was built up could have a tragic impact on future generations.

Chapter 7

Grassroots opinions

teachers' views concerning cause and intervention strategies

All teachers have a set of beliefs about what causes the problematic behaviour of some pupils, in just the same way that they will give reasons for the pro-social conduct of others. And individual teachers will construct, on the basis of the causal factors they attribute to the behaviour of children, an identity for the child based on the behaviour itself. How many times have you heard the expression 'He's a disruptive', or similar phrases which transmogrify an action into a human being? Attribution of cause and application of definition will inevitably proscribe the teaching and learning style adopted in the classroom. It is a truism that what teachers think about these matters will largely be a product of their heritage, mediated by factors relating to the internal and external demands placed on them in their present teaching post. This chapter explores some aspects of this complex issue, concentrating on teachers' beliefs about what causes problem behaviour and what are their preferred classroom interventions. In particular, it suggests that a preoccupation with definition is simply a management tool for the bureaucrat or administrator, rather than, as implied in the Code of Practice (DfE, 1994f), an important mechanism to meet the needs of pupils.

Wood for the trees? A rationale

The causes of problem behaviour are widespread, and have been briefly referred to elsewhere in this book. Cause cannot be separated from intervention. The beliefs that teachers hold about what makes children behave in the way they do will affect the kind of approach they adopt. This is as true of specific classroom interventions in problem behaviour as it is of a teacher's social interactions. If, for example, there is a belief that Boris's anti-social behaviour is a school-based manifestation of an alternative cultural style about which a teacher has no knowledge or empathy, it is likely that any problematic behaviour will be seen as oppositional to 'authority'. Such behaviour will be seen as challenging the established system, and is more likely to be met by an authoritarian, rule-governed stance than it is by a more open-minded, culturally aware strategy which might seek to incorporate elements of sub-culture within the functions of a school. This kind of individual and institutional response has been well-recorded in the literature, most recently by Sewell (1997).

On the other hand, a teacher may regard a particular instance of problematic behaviour as resulting from 'poor parenting' – which is rapidly assuming cult status as the scapegoat reason for the behaviour of pupils who do not conform to the educational or social ethic of Cool Britannia. Here there will undoubtedly be widespread calls for a punitive response, from both the individual school and its teachers or by the education system at large, and even more so by interest-groups driven by the prospect of political gain. Evidence of this, for example, is to be found in recent moves to 'punish' the parents of children who truant (*Times Educational Supplement*, 3. 4. 98). Alternatively, those schools and individual teachers who are familiar with, and recognise, the continued impact of a 'cycle of disadvantage' (Rutter and Madge, 1976) within education may be more likely to adopt strategies based on holistic intervention and collaboration.

Both of these projections are straightforward. But I have no wish to reduce to simplistic proportions the difficulties facing teachers in schools – particularly given that the pupils with problems land-scape has assumed an almost Napoleonic characteristic, whereby battles are being fought on several fronts. The pupils themselves are, in this situation, less of a 'problem' than the post-1988 context within which teachers have to operate, with its perpetual skirmishes with successive governments. Most notable has been the horse-trading, usually unacknowledged by teachers, exchanging de-centralisation of responsibility for centralisation of authority. Some of the themes generated by this stridently right-wing agenda, paradoxically, yet perhaps not inexplicably, being seamlessly maintained by New Labour, are illustrated and refined by the commentaries provided by teachers later in this chapter.

The approach that teachers adopt with pupils with problems will also vary according to how the term itself is defined. The prospect of defining this group of children and young people had already amplified the spectre of confusion to a state-of-the-art form by the 1970s. The Warnock Report (1978) formally recognised a group of pupils in schools who had 'emotional and behavioural disorders', signalling the possibility that the long-standing confusion over how to describe children whose behaviour in school was often difficult to manage may possibly be drawing to a close. But it was something of a false dawn, and the years following the 1981 Education Act have seen teachers and supporting professionals continuing to struggle with terminology. Even official documents signal the confusion. The *'Pupils with Problems'* circulars each relate to quite specific school-populations, although there are clearly definitional overlaps. The individual circulars themselves are littered with terms which attempt precise description, but almost invariably result in added confusion. Statements such as 'It may be argued... that every child has an emotional and behavioural difficulty of some kind at some point in their development, and that this is normal' (DfE, 1994b) are not helpful to teachers.

Like theories of causation, this terminological mayhem is very well documented (McCall and Farrell, 1993; Farrell, 1996). This is hardly surprising, given that the terms 'emotion' and 'behaviour' are amongst the most difficult concepts in the educational lexicon. Further difficulties arise because definitions of what comprise emotional and behavioural difficulty are closely bound up with the personality and professional experiences of the teacher who comes into contact with the pupil and by the influence of other professional orientations. Thus Hobbs (1978) confirmed that 'A particular child... may be regarded as mentally ill by a psychiatrist, as emotionally disturbed by a psychologist, and as behaviour-disordered by a special educator', whilst Upton (1983) agreed that 'Practitioners' preoccupation with more immediate issues frequently results in their assuming that (these) variations in terminology simply reflect different professional orientations, and that, in spite of differences in terminology, the basic conditions referred to by the terms are the same'.

Assessment-subjectivity is another problem. Compared to practice in the United States, where identification and assessment regimes for children with behaviour problems are both more sophisticated and prescriptive, an element of confusion remains. The Individuals with Disabilities Education Act (IDEA) is currently the primary federal law providing funding and policy guidance for the education of students with disabilities and was developed from its predecessor, Public Law 94-142 which was the North American counterpart of the 1981 Education Act. The latter, for example, did not recognise the term maladjustment, a descriptor which many workers in the field had long regarded as useful because it indicated a dysfunction between the individual and the society around him. As Kauffman (1984) later observed, 'The addition of that clause (excluding use of the term) makes the definition (serious emotional disturbance) nonsensical by any conventional logic... and is the kind of ambiguity of language and frailty of logic which keeps lawyers busy and drives decent people insane'.

Even following the adoption of IDEA it is clear that the teacher's task remains problematic, given that '...the statute applies only to students with learning problems based on a disability and not to students whose special needs stem from 'environmental, cultural or economic disadvantage'. These distinctions are not always easily made or even possible, given that such factors as prenatal nutrition and environmental pollution can lead to bona fide disabling conditions' (McDonnell, McLaughlin and Morison, 1997 p.55). In spite of such sweepingly detailed legislation, there remains in the United States a great deal of variability as to what is defined as 'emotional disturbance' and 'behaviour disorder' and in the way such disabilities are managed (McDonnell, McLaughlin and Morison, *op.cit.*)

England and Wales have witnessed similar confusion since the Warnock Report but without the precision afforded by DSM IV (the currently applicable diagnostic manual for educational psychologists in the USA), whatever its shortcomings. There is a growing belief that it is not necessarily appropriate for teachers working with pupils with problems to focus on definition (Gains and Garner, 1996). There has been a regrettable tendency to use definition to confirm prejudice and to assign provision, as in the case of the 'disruptive pupil', whilst the term 'maladjustment' provides a further illustration that definitions can simply be used to avoid confronting what might be quite painful institutional weaknesses in the approach to pupils with problems. To what is the pupil demonstrating a lack of adjustment? What if the system (the school) is inefficient, poorly organised and, in current parlance, 'failing'? What if the ethos of the school covertly supports the labelling of pupils? Is it not a good thing that the pupil is failing to adjust? Looked at from the perspective of school-improvement, there are powerful arguments for suggesting that a continued focus on what is 'wrong with the child' will deflect attention from those aspects of the school which are in all probability unsatisfactory for *all* children.

It may also be the case that a heavy emphasis on the categorisation of the anti-social behaviours by some pupils may deflect attention from their learning difficulties, an issue which the Warnock Report sought to remedy. Many teachers who have worked with pupils with problems would probably agree that much of the pupil behaviour regarded as 'disruptive' is a consequence of inappropriate curricula (Booth and Coulby, 1987). By using terms for the special needs of pupils which concentrate exclusively on their anti-social behaviour, positive action to deal with the real cause of the misbehaviour may not be taken.

When gathering the views of children who are termed disruptive it is clear that many of the suggestions they make concerning their education, whilst making sound sense, would be very difficult to implement (Garner, 1994). Whilst not wishing to be a conspiracy theorist, it nevertheless seems strange that, in this age of moral panic over standards of behaviour, very little money is being made available for the continuing professional development of those who work with EBD children. A cynical view may be also be taken of the underfunding which has accompanied the establishment of Pupil Referral Units and the demise of such establishments as Peper Harrow. In financial terms, it is less painful (for the Exchequer) to control young people by labels than it is to offer material assistance.

Finally, many teachers are actually disenchanted with continuing debates regarding definition and the discrepancies in what counts as 'emotional and behavioural difficulties' or 'pupils with problems' both from school to school and between LEAs. As one of my discussants (see below) has complained: '*A lot of time is spent in our place discussing the levels of offence* (sic) *and identifying descriptions for them. We spend a lot less time deciding what is best to do about it*' (Kathy). Frequently such debates exist at the expense of a much-needed focus on provision (whether in whole schools or individual classrooms). The omission of 'and provision' in the full title of the Code of Practice (*ibid*) is particularly regrettable in respect of EBD children, given the traditional marginalisation of this aspect of SEN. In assessing post-Elton Report initiatives, McManus (1989) has argued that the shortcomings of this way of thinking result in a position in which 'To rely upon definitions and categories to suggest remedies is to divert attention from observation of the individual and his or her circumstances. There are no easy solutions, so we have to think'.

Both 'cause' and 'definition' of the term 'pupils with problems' are irrefutably bound up with the personal response of a teacher and the intervention she uses to deal with the 'problem'. Her conceptualisation of these will have a relationship with what happens in the classroom. Nowhere is there more profound an illustration that 'the teacher is the key' (Weber, 1982). Acknowledgement of this relationship will allow the teacher to move away from the twin ills of definition disease and libelling by label.

A group of eight teachers, at present working in mainstream (primary and secondary), special schools and units, took part in a round-table discussion about their beliefs, working practices and views about likely future developments in the education of pupils with problems. All the teachers had posts of responsibility which brought them into regular official contact with these pupils; two worked in special (EBD) schools (Connie and Graham), one in a Pupil Referral Unit (Mandy), two as primary school SENCOs (Izzie and Evelyn) and three in secondary schools – one as SENCO and two as learning support teachers (Arthur, Kathy and Pete). The teachers met on two occasions, and the discussion was open ended, although topics were initially introduced by the author. The verbatim comments used in subsequent sections of this chapter have been abstracted from the transcripts taken during those times.

Some grassroots opinion: teachers' views concerning cause

The literature on causes of problem behaviour is arguably as substantial as that on intervention, with most recent studies identifying the usual suspects ranging from personality factors, through family and societal influences, to the effect of schools on children (see, for example, Sanders and Hendry, 1997). Thus, one respondent felt that *'There is not a lot a school can do when you're faced with wholesale chaos in the home'* (Izzie), whilst another felt that *'The major cause of difficulty is lack of cooperation with parents'* (Pete) and that *'Some kids have definitely got something wrong with them'* (Pete). It was noticeable that this type of remark was made more frequently by mainstream teachers during the discussions, suggesting that they may well be less accommodating of pupils with problems on account of other pressures.

From one point of view a preoccupation is understandable, given that an understanding of causation is likely to result in a strategic response, directed at the underlying reason for problem behaviour rather than the superficial symptoms. But dealing with causal factors as a kind of 'checklist' can lead to some unfortunate, if unintended, side-effects, notably in deficit-stereotyping and a failure to recognise 'ecological effect' (Bronfenbrenner, 1979). Thus,

Mandy felt that 'We are getting kids who to all intents and purposes are normal (sic); it's just that they have been tick-boxed out
of their school'. Because causal factors have largely remained
constant during the last thirty or so years, there is a danger that
we may simply feed off the historical evidence – thereby engaging
in a perverse form of self-fulfilment. Indeed, there may be some
suggestions that this phenomenon is being illustrated in this book,
most notably in Chapter 1, which has sought to confirm the
cyclical nature of disadvantage and, by inference, the profile and
background of a 'typical' pupil with problems.

Farrell (op.cit.), quoting Cooper (1993) provides an illustration of
this. In a section which dispatches causation in three pages and
ignores the impact of social factors, he summarises Cooper's
summary (yes) on home environment. The list is depressing,
including as it does such things as 'inconsistent parental discipline', 'parental use of corporal punishment', 'parental absences'
and 'violent temper displays from parents'. There may be times,
however infrequent, when a feeling of annoyance may become
something which could be placed in one of the aforementioned
categories. Under different social circumstances, performed by a
social actor whose cultural and economic capital is viewed as
'unsatisfactory', such actions would no doubt comprise a major
part of 'negative social factors' influencing behaviour. We need to
be aware of the minefield... Connie echoed this danger, noting
that 'Most of the kids we work with could, if the climate was
alright, be returned to mainstream schools. There behaviour is
frequently no worse than that of pupils at our feeder schools'.

I came from a 'good' family and a 'good' neighbourhood, in
which my abiding memory was one of love and selfless attention
to the needs of the children. Yet at least some of Cooper's
behaviours were manifest. In bluntly parading them in summary
form Farrell is in great danger of leading the reader (particularly
one who is embarking on a first journey through the literature) to
assume that such unwanted behaviours are continually present in
the family lives of pupils with problems. They are clearly not. It
would, in this instance, be worthwhile recalling the response

frequently given by the educational psychologists on being told by the teacher that 'Saddam is always fighting': 'Does he really fight all of the time?'. Or, as Graham observed, *'If we run sampling checks on a group of pupils we'll find that relatively few of them will behave badly all of the time... that's probably a physical impossibility anyway'*.

There has been a view, widely held, that many teachers subscribe to a deficit-orientation when allocating cause (Ford, Mongon and Whelan, 1982). As many commentators now recognise, such an individualised pathology is likely to result in a set of responses which divert attention from the real cause of alienation and dis-engagement. Arthur's rather cynical view of some of the pupils he works with bears this out: *'You can talk all you like about the effect of school... I think that if the kid is off the rails when he comes to you there is not much that you can do'*. Thankfully, there are suggestions that this way of thinking is being accom-modated within the professional ideology of those who work with pupils with problems. A snapshot series of comments from the teachers participating in the round-table lends support to this view, with Pete stating unreservedly that *'There are some things that we do as teachers which would annoy me if I was a pupil... I know... there is a lot of inconsistency which gets kids angry'*. Graham felt that *'...unless we look at what goes on inside the school then we will only be reinforcing the problems that these kids get in their day to day life'*, a point which was supported by Mandy: *'The (PRU) place is a haven for some of the kids. It's the only place where they are not going to be told they're wrong all the time'*.

Some grassroots opinion: how teachers work with pupils with problems

Much of the literature on EBD children refers to three types of intervention strategy, based on behavioural, psychodynamic or ecosystemic approaches. It is important to recognise that these strategies are not mutually exclusive. Most teachers will adopt a 'pick and mix' attitude to them, perhaps using parts of the behavioural approach alongside other practice, as the teacher-commentaries contained in this section of the chapter suggest. Only rarely will a whole school subscribe to one particular approach: such instances tend to be in special schools or units, where the size of the institution enables a single model to be used more easily. Furthermore, this brief overview presents merely the most common interpretation of each approach, there being many adaptations and derivatives, many of which are adjustments to local conditions in a given school.

i. Behavioural Approaches

The behavioural approach is based upon early theories of learning. Its proponents argue that, as all behaviour (good or bad) is learned, it can be unlearned. Typically this involves learning acceptable responses or unlearning responses which are not acceptable. It is also characterised by an emphasis on behaviours which are measurable (i.e. which can be observed) rather than upon the mental processes (causes) which prompt the behaviour in the first place. Consequently, formal assessment using time or event sampling, plays a crucial role prior to intervention. Many of the strategies subsequently adopted are well known, and figure to some extent in every teacher's practice: time-out, behaviour contracts, token economies and targeted punishment are good examples.

Behavioural approaches are an attractive proposition to teachers at present, given that much of the literature (and the hearsay evidence) suggests that they offer more hope of immediate impact than other interventions. Izzie said that 'We use behavioural approaches... though we don't call them that... mainly because of a lack of time and because we get little external support', also stating that 'It has been very successful in a short time span; we are pleased that we have committed ourselves to it'. Several other teachers in the discussion teachers found that this way of working has enabled them to develop effective interventions with 'problem children', as Kathy reports: 'I have found successes in using the behavioural approach – in setting targets for a whole class and for *an individual child. It shows that certain behaviours are the concern, not the child himself, and allows behaviour to be monitored and rewards given'.*

Nevertheless, the Warnock Report (1978) expressed concern about 'behaviour modification' used as an exclusive means of managing children, given that it implied that the teacher always knows best. Behavioural approaches continue to prompt feelings of suspicion, even hostility, amongst many teachers. One of the sources of uncertainty is the belief that intervening to change certain behaviours in children (and adults) seriously jeopardises the rights of the individuals concerned. Moreover, the argument is frequently made that, as an approach to human interaction, it is too simplistic and mechanistic, and is incapable of securing long-term improvements in difficult behaviour. Certainly there is some support for the view which suggests that using this approach relies upon external controls on behaviour; once these are removed the unwanted behaviours are likely to return.

Connie typifies these criticisms, remarking that *'My own reservations with regard to the behavioural approach is that it is based on extrinsic rewards. It is imposed on the child without true negotiation. It is not focusing on the context in which these behaviours are occurring. It distracts from the real causes of behaviour. Behaviour modification has already raised ethical questions regarding treatments used in attention deficit disorder'.* Her remarks need to be considered in a developing context of advocacy in special education in general, and with pupils with problems in particular (Garner and Sandow, *op.cit.*; Davie and Galloway, *op.cit.*). It may be argued that the child's participation in decision-making is a concept which has little relevance to extreme applications of behavioural intervention, such as assertive discipline (Canter and Canter, 1977), which are more akin to using mind-controlling drugs with troublesome pupils.

ii. Psychodynamic Approaches

This perspective adopts the view that problem behaviour has its source in the unconscious or sub-conscious thoughts of children.

It argues that even the earliest experiences of infants will have an effect on their emotional response to their environment. Psychodynamic theory originated with Freud, who sought to enable patients to review their 'life history' in order to reconstruct meanings for their present behaviour. For the EBD child, the psychodynamist argues, the inner world of emotions has remained largely unchanged since early childhood, resulting in a failure to adapt to the outer world. At the outset, however, it is important to preface this brief discussion with a word of caution. The approaches which might be considered under the collective heading of 'psychodynamic intervention' are numerous and often in themselves highly controversial. It is not the intention, in this brief section, to provide a survey of this huge field of activity; rather, the purpose is to obtain an intuitive feel for the perceptions of a group of teachers regarding the general orientation of this style of intervention.

Because strategies involving a psychodynamic orientation are extremely complex and usually require long-term training, there has been considerable reluctance, even prejudice, regarding its widespread adoption in educational settings. Evelyn felt that '...*because we are overloaded with other work the prospect of spending hours with a pupil discussing his past is totally unreasonable*'. A similar theme is identified by Arthur, who talks about the external pressures on him to 'get a result': '*If I was visited by an* (OFSTED) *inspector and I was not in full control of my class all of the time I'd be identified as failing; supposing I was just a few months into a therapeutic programme. Would the inspector understand that it takes time? I don't think so*'.

One understandable point of reluctance to become involved in the psychodynamic process is that many teachers (rightly) regard a child's emotional state as a kind of secret garden, into which only highly trained personnel can go. They have a fear that '...*suppressed feelings will be raised and they (teachers) will not have the necessary 'specialist' skills to deal with them. This will end up creating a lot of other concerns for the pupil so that, in the end, you have done more harm than good*' (Mandy).

In some ways it is reassuring that this group of teachers were reluctant to assume ownership of interventions that, by their own admittance, they knew very little about. There was a corresponding acceptance that, were the resources available – either through the allocation of trained counsellors to schools or by substantive, financially supported in-service training, then these kinds of interventions might be of more significance. Izzie summarised a collective viewpoint by stating that '*I think we all realise that many of our pupils have baggage they carry around, which influences their behaviour... these kinds of approaches could be helpful – but again it comes down to having to pay for something...*'. As psychodynamic approaches are invariably medium to long-term initiatives the net effect on a school is that a large slice of its training and support-service budget can be tied up, without guarantee of any amelioration in a child's behaviour, a point which found universal acceptance amongst the discussants.

iii. Ecosystemic Approaches

Those who support an ecosystemic view of problem behaviour would argue that all children belong to a set of sub-systems. Their behaviour (whether good or bad) is a product of interactions within and between these systems. Bronfenbrenner (1979) was highly influential in applying ecosystems to the study of human behaviour and, in particular, education. He argued that the world of the child comprised a *microsystem* (the child himself), the child and his teacher and classmates (the *mesosystem*), the child and his relationship to school as a whole and to parents and outside agencies (the *exosystem*), and finally the child in relation to the cultural, social and educational values and beliefs of the world in general (the *macrosystem*). Problematic behaviour occurs when there is a dysfunction between them.

Although not directly referring to education, Bronfenbrenner inferred that a successful exchange between teacher and child in any given setting would have benefits for the whole system, an issue of considerable importance to schools. The approach has subsequently become popular in the field of emotional and behavioural difficulties (Cooper, 1993; Ayers, Clarke and Murray, 1995) and is also strongly linked to the concept of school effectiveness. In the case of the latter one of the critical strategies for ensuring school success is the whole-school orientation; an ecosystemic approach to problem behaviour is precisely that, but without the rhetoric...

One of the advantages of the ecosystemic approach is that it prompts teachers to view the wider picture, and thus to examine the function of a pupil's behaviour in terms not just of the child himself but also in respect of the organisation as a whole. To recall a view expressed periodically throughout this book, it provides a major opportunity to create the conditions for a 'thinking school'. Izzie was enthusiastic about the potential of this approach: '...*if we can use it to get everyone thinking along the same lines then it would be excellent. I suppose what appeals to me is that senior management are not just involved to make the rules. They are as integral to what goes on as the behaviour of pupils themselves*'. Even Kathy, who had previously expressed strong opinions regarding the efficacy of behavioural approaches, felt that the ecosystemic orientation had something to offer: '*Environments, expectations and interactions must equally be considered in assessing behaviour. If we wish to alter behaviour we need to consider changes to all aspects rather than assuming the child has a problem*'.

There is, within the ecosystemic approach, a fairly explicit commitment to inter- and intra-professional cooperation. This, however, may be the model's Achilles heel, in view of the resource implications that such activities imply. The teachers participating in this discussion were quick to point this out: Pete felt that '*The chances of making things work even within a school are limited because of lack of time. I have trouble getting free time to see an EWO (education welfare officer) even now; would we be given time to make the links that this theory suggests?*'.

Some tentative conclusions...

The brief extracts from the teachers in this chapter provide evidence of debate concerning cause and intervention. The teachers supported intensive but high-cost programmes involving psychotherapy and inter-professional collaboration. This enthusiasm is tempered with a pragmatic view of what is reasonable for teachers to achieve at the present time, when '...*all we seem to hear about is funding cuts. They seem to want to take every single form of external support we've got*' (Arthur). It seems safe to assume that most teachers will continue to seek examples of approaches that work in the classroom, and do so with some immediacy. In using such interventions it is clear, from this small group of teachers at least, that they will avoid a slavish adherence to a single approach, preferring to select a combination of theories which, in their professional judgment, might work best. As Kathy remarked, effective work with pupils with problems needs to be '...*flexible and uncluttered by prejudice in choosing one technique rather than another*'.

Three tentative inferences may be drawn from the foregoing: each is worth further investigation, particularly given the climate of criticism that teachers now work in and the increasing emphasis being given to pupils with problems, as displayed by *Excellence for all Pupils*. Firstly, the five mainstream teachers generally perceived specialist techniques (like psychodynamic interventions) for managing behaviour as being very limited in their own classrooms. They believe them to be largely unworkable without considerable investment of personnel and in further, ongoing professional development.

Secondly, and more particularly, teachers in all schools show an ability to adapt, revise or combine elements of the approaches described, a view supported by Hanko (1985). In consequence it is essential that some thought is given to programmes which enable teachers to draw the most relevant, workable and defensible practices from each, both for themselves and the children they teach.

Thirdly, there is a suggestion that teachers working in mainstream settings may now be less tolerant of the behaviour of certain pupils; where teachers feel that the 'blame' for certain kinds of behaviour belongs in the home, or in the child, there may be less inclination on their part to do something about it and they are more likely to adopt a more punitive response to the pupils concerned.

The debate concerning the causes of problem behaviour and the interventions which teachers adopt will surely continue. In participating it seems essential that the less partisan and precious teachers can be about particular approaches, and the more open they are to research evidence concerning causal factors, then the more likely it is that successful outcomes can be achieved for pupils with problems (and their teachers).

Chapter 8

Involving pupils in managing behaviour

The last twenty years or so has witnessed a gradual rise in the importance of understanding and listening to the viewpoints of the young person who has Special Educational Needs (SEN). An interest in gathering the viewpoint of the 'consumer' has been apparent in many aspects of education. In educational research, for instance, Armstrong, Galloway and Tomlinson (1993) have charted three areas of activity, noting work in classroom ethnography (Woods, 1979), motivational style (Rogers, 1982) and curriculum development (Bond and Compas, 1989). These, and other, researchers began the process of placing a new emphasis upon the pupils' 'reality', in what Bronfenbrenner (1979) has referred to as the 'ecosystem', in which everyone involved in a given context is viewed as an active participant in its processes and events. Subsequently there has been an outpouring of literature on the theme, perhaps indicative of a historical failure to recognise the crucial importance of pupils as informants. Some aspects of this body of literature are discussed elsewhere in this chapter.

In practical terms the use of pupils' views has begun to be widely advocated across a wide range of school activity relating to SEN (Cooper, 1993; Davie and Galloway, 1995; Garner and Sandow, 1995; Smith, 1998). Such a participatory approach to the organisation and management of schools stands in stark contrast to what has been the case in education. Gribble (1993), for instance, summarised both adult and professional fears concerning the dangers of allowing young people a platform, stating that 'Children are more honest. They have not learnt our hypocrisy. That is why it hurts so much when they tell us what we ought to do, and we know they are right' (p.8). Few of those who work with pupils with problems, whether they have learning difficulties or not, would argue that they are inclined to shy away from 'telling it like it is'.

Developments in research and practice have been heavily influenced by changing policy orientations in SEN. These have led towards an assumption on the part of many teachers that children have something valuable to say about what happens to them in school. The principle has been applied across a range of professional activities in respect of SEN. Burden and Hornby (1989), for example, warned that 'One of the biggest mistakes that the system orientated school psychologist can make is to neglect the views of the customers – the pupils'.

Several important developments, both nationally and internationally, have charted the way for some change towards a new practice of 'listening to children'. The United Nations Convention on the Rights of the Child (1989) embodies a number of principles which, hitherto, had largely been lacking in this field. Freeman (1987) remarked that pupils had frequently been 'denied the status of participants in the social system, labelled as a problem population, reduced to being seen as property'. The UN Convention clearly articulated a changing view, wherein 'The child capable of forming their own views shall be assured the right to express those views freely, on all matters affecting him or her, and these will be given weight in accordance with the child's age' (Article 12).

1989 also witnessed the Children Act in England and Wales, which sought to enshrine the spirit of the U.N. Convention. Prior to this there was evidence, in the legislation relating to SEN, of a good deal of rhetoric where the views of young people were concerned. Thus, whereas Circular 22/89 of the 1981 Education Act stated that 'Older children and young persons should be able to share in discussions on their needs and any proposed provision' (p.7), and that 'The feelings and perceptions of the child should be taken into account and the concept of partnership should, wherever possible, be extended...'(para. 17), there remained, by the end of the 1980's, ample evidence that the pupil participation in decision-making was, at best, marginal (Gersch, Holgate and Sigston, 1993).

But much of the rhetoric, and the practice that it inspired, tacitly concerned only the pupils whose SEN did not involve 'problematic' behaviours of the kinds being considered in this book. For example, Wade and Moore (1993) make little or no mention of children with emotional and behavioural difficulties in what was one of the first books devoted to the perspective of the child with SEN. The Elton Report (1989) at least acknowledged that pupils did have a viewpoint, recommending that '...headteachers and teachers should encourage the active participation of pupils in shaping and reviewing the school's behaviour policy in order to foster a sense of collective commitment to it' (p.144). It also emphasised that teachers should '...give pupils every opportunity to take responsibilities and to make a full contribution to improving behaviour in schools'. But these exhortations flattered to deceive; the Elton Report comprised over 130 recommendations, most of which reinforced a control ethic rather than one of enablement. Thus, it was noted that there tended to be a focus upon 'managing' the behaviour of those who had what were described as emotional and behavioural problems rather than understanding the feelings of such pupils (DES, 1989). Little attention was paid to the involvement of pupils with problems in anything other than their own behaviour – school procedures, the curriculum and the way in which teachers themselves behaved were explicitly ignored.

The Code of Practice (DfE, 1994) affirms that 'special educational provision will be most effective when those responsible take into account the ascertainable wishes of the child concerned' (p.3). The Code focuses mainly upon the identification and assessment of special needs. Its recommendation to schools that they should involve pupils in decision-making processes needs to be given wider currency, so that it covers more general whole-school matters, including policies relating to discipline, curriculum, school organisation and so on.

Circular 8/94, entitled 'Pupil Behaviour and Discipline' (DfE, 1994), tacitly reaffirms the official view that pupils should be involved in the development of schools' behaviour policies. In stating that 'They should be worked out cooperatively' (p.3) the circular is reinforcing the advice promoted by the Elton Report (1989) that the views of pupils should be taken into account in matters relating to school discipline. Once again, however, there is little other encouragement to be obtained from the Pupils with Problems Circulars for this approach. It would appear that its inclusion was almost an afterthought, born more out of political correctness than from social justice.

It is noticeable that all three official documents (the Elton Report, the Code of Practice and Circular 8/94) stop short of recommending that pupils should, as a matter of course, be involved in helping to make decisions about school policy. These publications do represent a step forward, in seeing children who have special needs not as 'fixed', uni-dimensional individuals but as active agents in their own school lives. So there is, therefore, a perceptible change in attitude towards including pupils' views. Whilst this may fall short of an ideal situation for pupils with problems, who are traditionally seen as a separate case, there now exists some statutory guidance on involving pupils in what happens to them in school.

Moreover, the ways in which pupil-opinion is sought, assimilated and acted upon is now recognised as an indicator of school-effectiveness, signalled, for example, in Framework 4 of the school inspection manual, which uses the question 'Do the school's arrangements encourage all pupils to contribute to school life and to exercise responsibility?' (OFSTED, 1993). Whilst there is an elegant pragmatism about such a question (few teachers would directly seek to contradict the content of the inspection schedules...), it acts as a further stimulus to schools to seek out pupil viewpoints. In the case of pupils with problems, the inclusion of the phrase 'all pupils' is especially potent.

Can the involvement of pupils with problems be justified?

In the light of the debate after the publication of the Green Paper, *Excellence for All*, and of the militant stance adopted by some teacher unions to the inclusion of EBD pupils in mainstream schools (NAS/UWT, 1998), this statement should not be regarded as unproblematic. Nevertheless it presents an indication that, at national level, there is now a recognition that the views of those who have special needs can be of positive benefit to schools in policy-development. This is at least implied by some of the official statements referred to earlier in this chapter.

This having been said there are particular problems associated with pupil involvement in policy-making, particularly where some of those who need to be involved are seen as 'problems'. Pupils who have learning difficulties associated with 'problem behaviour' frequently conjure up negative feelings in many teachers (Hargreaves, Hestor and Mellor, 1975). This is understandable. Being a teacher is not easy at a time when undue emphasis is placed on outputs, measured by normative indicators such as examination success, exclusion and truancy rates, measurable progress from one National Curriculum attainment target to the next and so on. Moreover, as teachers now operate in a climate of increasing accountability, in which a failure to perform may result in the wrath of Chris Woodhead or one of his frenzied acolytes, many teachers, particularly in mainstream schools, may be less than inclined to listen to what pupils with problems have to say.

An examination of the recent literature on pupil-involvement will go some way towards reassuring those who doubt the merits of this approach. Both the intrinsic, ethical worth of listening to pupils and the more pragmatic institutional development outcomes of the process are apparent. Whilst there has been a marked increase in the amount of literature devoted to the views of pupils during the 1980s, it is probably fair to suggest that only a small amount of this has related to pupils with problems. Schostak (1983) indicates that this may be a view that 'disruptive' pupils are of less importance because they benefit schools least. Nonetheless the 1980s did see the beginnings of literature in the field, with O'Hagan and Edmunds (1982), Dawson (1984) and Scarlett (1989) all providing examples of research which sought to uncover pupils' views on their educational experiences. A good deal of this work concerns the pupil's view of his teachers. Thus Scarlett (*op.cit.*) showed that so-called disruptive pupils regarded such qualities as 'fairness' and 'respect' as vital teacher-characteristics. Meanwhile Getzels and Smilansky (1983) noted that 'The predominant observation regarding the content of problems seen by pupils is the 'unfair' and 'uncaring' behaviour of teachers'.

The 1990s have witnessed something of a consolidation of this earlier work. Whilst much of the literature in this more recent period relates to SEN in general (Davie and Galloway, 1995; Moore and Wade, 1993; Garner and Sandow, 1995), there have been encouraging signals that the views of pupils are seen both as vital data components in research concerning pupils with problems (Cooper, 1993) but also as a source of insight which can lead to practical innovations (Garner, 1992; Jones and Charlton, 1996; Schools Councils UK, 1995).

Such small-scale findings accord with the official views on the expected qualities of teachers. The DES, for instance, argues that teachers should be able to establish positive relationships with their classes based on mutual respect (DES, 1989). More recently this theme has been highlighted by OFSTED (1996), in its school inspection frameworks.

If we look briefly to the United States it is apparent that similar developments, more in advance of England and Wales, have been taking place. Building on the work of such researchers as Stallworth, Frechtling and Frankel (1983) and Murtaugh and Zeitlin (1989), Stevenson (1991) and Furtwengler (1990) have presented two vital theories in the quest to secure respectability for the (problem) pupil-involvement movement: the Collective Resource Perspective (CRP) and Reaching Success through Involvement (RSI).

The guiding principle of CRP is that, whilst the managerial perspective tends to view deviant students (here using the preferred

US-term for high school pupils) as detrimental to the quality of classroom life, the use of disruptive (*sic*) students as a resource allows the development and enforcement of rules via negotiation. In advocating this approach Stevenson (*op.cit.*) suggested that the students can promote order by helping to clarify, in the students' own terms, the goals of the classroom and the rules which govern them.

RSI is based on the initial involvement of students in a 'school retreat', where teachers and both official and 'informal' student-leaders formed action teams to identify problems relating to school discipline. Each action team worked throughout the year on individual school discipline problems – these ranged from persistent lateness to the students' complaint that they were not given opportunities to have their say. Subsequently the teams produced 'profiles' of what comprised 'good' teachers and students. One difficulty, identified by Furtwengler (*op.cit.*) was the time it took some teachers to accept an apparent loss of 'control' in decision-making.

What does pupil participation look like?

Pupil participation in schools can be at a variety of levels. But there is a real danger that their involvement is only in those areas which have, at best, little impact on the organisation and the way it operates – typically illustrated by pupil 'councils' which do nothing more than offer advice about school uniform or lunch-time menus. Pupils with problems should, as a matter of course, be involved in substantive matters relating to their time in school. These include involvement in:

- policy-making

- school organisation

- curriculum and pedagogy

- management of behaviour.

In order to do this schools have to make strategic decisions in four areas, recognising that the overall process will not comprise short term initiatives nor short term gains. Firstly, a school climate has to be nurtured in which cooperation and shared decision-making between pupils and teachers is seen as routine rather than exceptional. Developing this requires an examination of existing attitudes within the school, especially those management practices which affect the way teachers do their job and the way in which children learn. As indicated in Chapter 4, this process is a challenging one, but it is an essential basis from which to begin. Typically this might take the form of an 'audit' of views – both from pupils and teachers, concerning aspects of school life. One secondary school I know organised such a survey based on the OFSTED framework for inspection, thus covering such aspects as attitudes, behaviour and personal development, leadership and management, accommodation, learning resources and so on.

Identifying the gap that exists between policy and practice, and the different interpretation of them by teachers and pupils, allows insight into possible points for action. This constitutes the next stage of the process. Crucially, the decisions on what is or is not important are not then the preoccupation solely of the teachers, and particularly those in senior management positions. Identification of *foci* for action and the targets to be reached in each should be as much part of the process as 'data' collection itself, and should again be characterised by pupil-involvement. The importance in creating the conditions for this to take place immediately becomes apparent; once more it is worth remembering that the 'thinking' school is not created overnight...

Thirdly, the pupils themselves need to be given the skills and strategies necessary to enable them to present their views of their school experience in a rational, assertive and objective way. The development of these skills, which has been so much under threat in the era of post-1988 curricular prescription, is an essential part of the jigsaw, providing the necessary equipment for pupil-participation in a more democratically run school (Brandes and Ginnis, 1990).

Finally, everyone in the school has to be given the opportunity to engage in planning, implementing and reviewing at each point at which action is seen as necessary. This is the pivot, of course, and an assessment of whether the school has been able to shift its approach to pupils with problems, by utilising 'thinking' school mechanisms, to become a democratic institution will largely depend upon its activities and outputs in this respect. Whilst not referring directly to this 'staged' approach, an illuminating analysis, together with accompanying exemplars, of the process of utilising pupil opinion is contained in Jones and Charlton (*op.cit.*).

Involving the pupil: examples from the four stages

Each of the four stages described in the previous section is illustrated in this part of the chapter by case-study examples which draw upon small-scale research activity. That one of the examples uses comparative data is indicative of the need, hinted at earlier, that we should not remain parochial in our search for good practice. Moreover, it may act as a reassurance that problem behaviour by pupils is not solely a concern for teachers in England and Wales...

i. Gauging the ethos for participation

In this example the views of 12 boys, aged between 14 and 16 years, from each of three schools were sought, using a semi-structured conversation schedule. The boys were selected in each case by the headteacher of the school; they could read a transcript of what they had said, and delete anything with which they did not agree. The schools were located in very different political, social and cultural settings, with the commensurate impact on the education systems concerned. One school (subsequently identified in this section by the initials US) was located in the Pacific North-West of the United States; it had 65 pupils on roll aged between 12-16 years. A high proportion (23) of these had been placed in the school by social welfare agencies. Only a small number were girls (7), though there was an over-representation of native-American Indians (6). The school was well equipped, and provided a curriculum based on the liberal arts, vocational subjects and social skills. The English special school (subsequently identified in this section by the initial E) was located in the North West of England, and had 47 pupils on roll, aged between 11-16 years. The school was an independent, self-governing school which admitted pupils who were referred from 11 LEAs. Only 9 of the pupils were girls, and there was an over-representation of children from minority groups, notably Black African-Caribbean (8). The school provided a curriculum which was based entirely upon the existing National Curriculum. The third school, situated in the North-West of Bulgaria (subsequently identified in this section by the initial B), catered for 300 pupils and an age-range from 3-16 years. Over 70% of the children were categorised as being of gypsy-origin. The school provided both a primary- and secondary-age Bulgarian national curriculum for all its pupils, apart from the 36 kindergarten children. Each of the schools was residential and designated for children described variously as having 'emotional disturbance' (US) 'emotional and/or behavioural difficulties' (E) or 'maladjustment problems' (B).

The interview schedule focused on four aspects of the boys' experience in school: the curriculum and its delivery; the personal and professional qualities of teachers; the pupils' own interpretations of disruptive behaviour; and the organisation and ethos of the school (see Figure 1). The statements made by the pupils were categorised as being either positive (+) or negative (-) by the researcher and the headteachers from each of the three schools. Two visits were made to each case-study site, and, in the case of the Bulgarian example, the conversation with pupils utilised the services of a translator who had no official connection with the school.

Figure 2 provides a summary of the pupil statements in each of the four categories of school experience under consideration in each special school. Although a quantitative summary is provided for illustration the study sought to place an emphasis upon the individual pupil's 'reality', as indicated by their comments during the conversations. Their commentaries are intended to illustrate the potential for incorporating the views of young people in schools, whether mainstream or segregated.

CURRICULUM AND ITS DELIVERY

Can you tell me something about the lessons you have in school?
What school subject do you like/dislike most of all?
What sort of learning activity do you enjoy?
What sort of things do you dislike doing in class?
What do you do if you are unable to do the work in class?

PERSONAL & PROFESSIONAL QUALITIES OF TEACHERS

Tell me something about your teachers.
Which teacher(s) do you get on well with? Why do you think this is?
Which teacher(s) don't you get on with? Why?

INTERPRETATIONS OF DISRUPTIVE BEHAVIOUR

What sort of things have got you into trouble in school?
Which do you think was the most serious behaviour?
Who's fault do you think it was?
Do you think that the punishment was fair?
How do you think that the school should have handled behaviour problems?

SCHOOL ORGANISATION AND ETHOS

Do you enjoy being in school?
What is the best/worst thing about it?
What do you think about the rules which schools make for students?
What is the thing which you will most remember about being in school?

Figure 1: The Semi-Structured Conversation Schedule

Figure 2: Positive and Negative Comments from 'Disruptive' Students

| | NUMBER OF COMMENTS | | | | | | % + Comments | | |
	England		USA		Bulgaria		E	US	B
CONVERSATION TOPIC	+	−	+	−	+	−	E	US	B
Curriculum	41	60	38	42	40	29	41	47	58
Qualities of Teachers	52	41	46	41	60	16	56	53	79
Interpretations of Disruptive Behaviour	32	54	39	51	52	22	37	43	70
School Organisation & Ethos	37	62	30	37	67	19	37	45	78
TOTAL*	162	217	153	171	219	86			

* 52 comments were classified as neither + or −

It is important to recognise that the pupils often expressed very positive views about their school situation. Whilst positive comment was in the overall minority, especially in the schools in England and the United States, the data indicates that such pupils are far from negative about what happens to them in school. They also indicate very rational interpretations about their experiences. Such an outcome may have important implications for institutional and professional development.

The pupils' comments relating to curriculum showed that they invariably acknowledged their learning difficulties ('I get into trouble for giving teachers cheek. But I don't understand the stuff and I just get mad' E; 'Some of the stuff we do in class is sick, man. It's no good to me. Either it's too hard or my kid sister could do it' US; 'When I don't understand anything I ask to go to the doctor to get out of it' B)

There remained, however, evidence of considerable enthusiasm for learning activity ('I work hard in most of my lessons because I enjoy them' E; 'I try hard to get on with my work so's I'll get a good job' US; 'If I don't understand I will read it once, twice, until I do understand' B). Such positive attitudes to schoolwork indicate a good deal of insight by the pupils into their own learning style. The suggestion here is that, contrary to some opinion, young people who are categorised as being 'pupils with problems' are capable of critical self-evaluation.

The research also indicates that the pupils are able to offer reflective and balanced comment concerning the personal and professional qualities of their teachers. Moreover, the pupils imply that they are able to sense that a wider set of issues, often out of the control of their teachers, can impinge upon their education ('My school hasn't got enough teachers, so everyone is too busy' E; 'When teachers are on supervisory duty they are human; you can talk to them then' US; 'The teacher is not always available because he's got lots of other things to do' B).

Certain characteristics also seem to be highlighted by the pupils as being of particular importance in stimulating learning. Amongst these the need for a sense of humour figures frequently, and corresponds to the social process of 'having a laugh' (Woods, 1979): 'I think that Mrs .... is best because she's nice and because she's got a sense of humour inside her' E; 'All the guys in the group prefer teachers who can control the class and let us have a laugh' US; 'When we do something wrong the teacher has to understand that it's sometimes a joke' B. A range of other qualities which they looked for in teachers were noted by the pupils: these included clarity of instruction, good discipline, fairness and approachability.

The young people in this study express forthright opinions concerning issues of school discipline and their own involvement in problematic behaviours. They nevertheless remain remarkably balanced in their observations. The pupils' interpretations of disruptive incidents suggested that, whilst on the one hand they often maintained high expectations of school behaviour ('If you mess about in class you deserve to get sent out' E; 'The worst offence is causing trouble in the class so that other kids can't reach their grades' US; 'We don't like bad behaviour of any sort' B), they were nevertheless critical of the lack of consultation on issues of discipline ('No-one pays any attention to us. We get treated like shit' E; 'We should have a hand in the (Discipline) Codes' US).

Little negative comment was forthcoming on this question from the Bulgarian pupils, as Figure 2 illustrates. This may point to certain socio-cultural and political differences between England and the United States on the one hand and Bulgaria on the other. In fact it is accurate to point out that, in each of the four aspects of school experience under consideration, the Bulgarian pupils expressed more positive than negative comment. This situation may be indicative of the newly-emerging democratic processes within Bulgarian society in general, in which individuals have not been used to publicly expressing their opinions. It may also be suggestive of the fact that, in Bulgaria, special schools for those who are termed 'maladjusted' serve an crucial social function, given that this part of the special school population is drawn almost exclusively from the families of the economically poor or from minority cultural and ethnic groups (notably the country's gypsy population). Comments by the Bulgarian pupils which are indicative of this are that ' I sometimes feel bad when I have to go on holiday because I miss school' B, and ' We like it here because it's warm and we get food' B.

Finally, the young people in all three schools expressed broadly similar opinions concerning aspects of school organisation and ethos. A stress was placed by them on social interactions with both their teachers and peers, and upon the school procedures which facilitated these ('I enjoy this school because you can relax with your friends and the teachers make time to talk to you' E; 'This school's OK. It treats you OK. The teachers care a lot and make time for us' US; 'The best thing is we're all together here. After finishing teaching the teachers play games with us' B).

In sum, therefore, the young people who were the subject of this small-scale research express opinions about school which, whilst frequently negative, contain significant number of positive comments. There is also some evidence that, in spite of substantial historical, social and cultural differences between the three countries considered, there remains a number of areas of broad agreement on matters concerning their education.

The views of the pupils reported in this section of the chapter carry a number of important implications for both school organisation and for the professional training and practice of teachers. These can be traced in each of the four groups of pupil-response. At the outset, too, it is worth noting that the views expressed by these pupils appear to be little different from those provided by the more normative school populations (Raymond, 1987). There is also a suggestion that these views are similar to those held by the teachers themselves; in this instance the pupils are acting as a mirror in which a teacher can show her own practice, thus hinting at a further opportunity for professional development.

In matters relating to the school curriculum the pupils highlight the need to make their studies both flexible and responsive to their future needs. This is a point of some contention in England, where the programmes of study and the assessment procedures which accompany them, have been established as a formal part of the

National Curriculum. It has been argued (Fordham, 1989) that a formalised National Curriculum should not mean the diminution of the right of those with SEN to have access to a broad and balanced range of learning activities. A contrary view, however, has been expressed by Mittler (1992) who maintained that '... we are bound to ask whether the National Curriculum will seriously address the large achievement gap between children from different social backgrounds'. Whatever the outcome of this debate, it is clear that the pupils themselves have an important contribution to make in its resolution.

The need to develop new skills in teacher assessment, differentiation of curriculum material and teaching and learning styles is a high priority. Unfortunately the 'battle' has to be fought in a new, market-driven educational environment, wherein those pupils whose SENs relate to their perceived problem-behaviour may be further disadvantaged (Reynolds, 1989). Teacher education in England, too, has come under brutal scrutiny by the present Government, so that 'at a stroke the work of the last ten years' (Mittler, 1992), in which all new teachers received a compulsory SEN element in their initial training, will have been cancelled. It is therefore in some doubt whether the English system of training can provide an effective model for teacher training or development in curricular areas of SEN.

The pupils in this study have suggested that they recognise certain desirable qualities in their teachers. Not least of these are fairness and a sense of humour. It may be that more time should be devoted, in both pre-service and professional development settings, to work which enables teachers to empathise more readily with their pupils: in the present environment such approaches are all but impossible, given the fanatical manner in which professional development funds are being directed towards such things as assessment, basic skills and core curriculum subjects. Moreover, the data forthcoming from this kind of exercise has important implications for the selection and use of staff from special schools for leading training activities for mainstream teachers who may work with pupils with problems. It also suggests that more emphasis should be placed on the way in which prospective teachers are selected for training courses, so that personality factors, identified by these pupils as being of crucial importance, might be explored in far greater detail than hitherto.

The important issue of democracy is highlighted by the young people in this study. They indicate a desire to participate more fully in the way the schools deal with them. This will require a shift in emphasis, away from an unquestioning view that schools serve the needs of society and, as such, have tended to belong to teachers rather than pupils. There is a need to establish the importance of self-advocacy on the part of pupils, so that their views can provide insights and possible solutions 'to all the issues that underlie any school, from the curriculum to teacher appraisal' (Cullingford, 1991).

The essential paradox is that, whilst the pupils in this study are arguing for more time to be spent with their teachers, for less prescriptive teaching, access to decision-making processes and for the establishment of more effective social relationships, the current demands for change in the education systems of all three countries, in order that their education systems may respond to a market-driven ideology, may mean the continued marginalisation and isolation of the young person. In other words, pupils who have emotional and behavioural difficulties will be unable to participate fully in the educational context of which they are the focus.

The example I have provided relates to segregated settings. I have replicated the same process with a group of pupils and teachers in mainstream schools (Garner, 1993). In each case the teachers themselves recognised the value of 'listening to pupils', in that it often enabled them to see beyond what had hitherto been a blind-spot or an assumption about the merits of the status quo. The process of gathering the views of pupils (alongside those of the teachers and others) was viewed, in hindsight, as a far less threatening activity than had been imagined. As one teacher in the English special school observed, 'This has opened my eyes to what really goes on... our kids think along the same lines as us on a lot of things'.

ii. Identifying the gap that exists between policy and practice

There is a not unreasonable assumption that policy is invariably 'made' by teachers and practice is 'experienced' by pupils. The former is a representation, from the point of view of teachers (or, more especially, a certain group of teachers) of the 'ideal state' in which the educational endeavour should take place. In practice such visions may be somewhat inadequate from the perspective of the young people on the receiving end.

iii. Developing the skills and strategies for participation

Children who have special educational needs associated with problem behaviour are often described as lacking in social skills. As a result they frequently get into trouble with teachers and other pupils because they respond inappropriately in certain social situations (Rogers, 1992). They are unfamiliar with many of the sophisticated codes and protocols which govern life in schools. This in turn may militate against their successful involvement in new processes.

So we need to enable all pupils, and especially those who have learning difficulties associated with problem behaviour, to negotiate with their teachers and peers. Broadly speaking negotiation involves such skills as listening, managing conflict, assertiveness training, taking risks, accepting responsibility and dealing with feelings.

Many pupils who have learning difficulty find these skills very challenging, for a variety of reasons. Many will find it very difficult to accept responsibility for their actions, even, when they may clearly be the perpetrators ('It wasn't me, Miss ....'). Others may have a very low self-opinion, and consequently believe that there is little point in stating a point of view. Still more may be so accustomed to failure that they may be unwilling to participate in anything which might expose their weaknesses. In the most extreme cases, several of these may overlap, contributing to the child being either excessively withdrawn or aggressive.

Additionally, just as it has been noted that teachers occupy roles which are dictated by tradition, so too, many children in schools (and especially those with special educational needs) see themselves as parts of a system over which they have no real control. Building up the confidence and trust, so that participation in rule-making and policy matters is seen as axiomatic, requires long-term commitment on the part of all teachers in a school. As with the process of creating a 'climate' in which pupil-participation will flourish, it does not happen by itself – it has to be planned.

If a school wishes to promote pupil participation, so that there is benefit in teaching and learning to everyone in the school, such programmes need a high priority. Part of the risk-taking on the part of senior management teams is that such programmes should be maintained at all costs, irrespective of National Curriculum requirements or other pressures. The enhancement of pupils' learning and teachers' teaching can far outweigh the time 'lost' in promoting these cooperative strategies.

iv. Planning, Implementing and Reviewing

The Cliff School is a mixed, 11-16 comprehensive school, under LEA control, situated in a medium-sized town in the South Midlands. The school has 570 pupils on roll and 41 teachers. It has a catchment area mainly comprising two large estates, one of which is predominantly homes of owner-occupiers; the second, smaller estate has been the focus of some local difficulties, with a number of street disturbances, incidents of joy-riding and a residual population with a high proportion of single-parent families, unemployment, delinquency and overcrowded accommodation. The school occupies a site to the north of the town centre, with buildings dating mainly from the mid-1970s.

The internal organisation of the school is based on fairly traditional lines, with a headteacher (male), two deputy headteachers and nine heads of subject departments, two of which now function on a school-wide basis as 'Literacy Coordinator' and 'Numeracy Coordinator'. Pastoral arrangements are overseen by one of the deputies, who is supported by a Head of Lower School and a Head of Upper School. The school has a moderate local reputation, competing in the locality with both a boys' and a girls' high school (grant maintained) and an independent school. The school's most recent OFSTED inspection (1995) revealed weaknesses in 'some aspects of school organisation' and in 'the management of pupil behaviour'.

Following the early retirement of the previous incumbent a newly appointed headteacher, Linda Ilsam, together with a new deputy headteacher, presented a series of initiatives to the staff relating to pupil behaviour. It was her view that, unless the issue of pupil misbehaviour, both in and out of lessons, was addressed the school would be unable to deal with the poor performance of a large group of pupils. Both issues, she concluded in her discussion document to staff, were major barriers to presenting the school as a reasonable alternative to its grant-maintained counterparts. A 'school review' was undertaken which, significantly, included input from parents, pupils and the local community. 'Unacceptable behaviour' by some pupils was identified by each of these groups as the most pressing problem facing the school. Dealing with this issue was to be a central focus of the Cliff School's Five Year Plan. The principal concern was a group of pupils in Year 10, who many teachers felt were alienated from the aims of the school.

After conversation with several members of the school's pastoral team, the new deputy headteacher, Robin Keith, said that some staff felt that at least part of the problem could be traced to the lack of involvement in decision-making felt by a group of Year 10 boys. A preliminary questionnaire survey of the whole of the school had revealed that almost a third of pupils felt they did not have a say in making curriculum choices or in the development of the school's discipline policy; nor did they feel that they were part of the social life of the school. In addition, some pupils viewed certain subjects and teachers as 'boring'. There was a high level of 'internal truancy', which the boys confided was their means of demonstrating opposition whilst relieving boredom. These views were far more apparent amongst the boys, and particularly so amongst boys in Year 9 and to an even greater extent in Year 10. A further questionnaire, directed towards these two year groups, was distributed; these were to be completed in the children's own time, in confidence, and their return was voluntary; of a total number of 228 pupils 219 questionnaires were returned, a response rate of 96%. An opportunity was then made available to all Year 9 and Year 10 pupils to discuss aspects of school organisation, in the broadest sense. On five subsequent occasions one deputy headteacher and the Head of Upper School had a discussion with the pupils about five key areas, that had been identified by the pupils, (a) the curriculum (b) school discipline (c) the school as a social place (d) the school in the community and (e) teachers and pupils.

The views of the pupils, expressed both in questionnaire format and in the discussions, provided their teachers with a remarkable insight into the process of schooling. It was, for some staff '*A startling experience. It was the first time that they had ever been put under the microscope and I think that some were genuinely shocked with what they saw*' (Linda Ilsam). The results of the questionnaire and some extracts from the discussions were subsequently distributed to all pupils. They indicated that many pupils in the school were acutely aware of what are the necessary professional qualities for teachers to possess, demonstrating a remarkable overlap with some of the 'desirable attributes' of newly qualifying teachers, as contained in the current guidance to providers of initial teacher education (DfEE, 1997). The pupils valued teachers who appeared to work hard and were well-prepared for lessons and who 'treated us with respect' whilst maintaining a sense of humour. Moreover, there was overwhelming support for teachers who dispensed 'firm but fair discipline' and who explained exactly why they were sanctioning a pupil.

Robin Keith expressed little surprise at these findings, but felt that the process thus far had not 'reached' a group of Year 10 pupils who seemed to him to be at the centre of '*potentially difficult situations or even outright disruption in class*' (Robin Keith). The next stage of the initiative therefore involved this group of 9 pupils, all boys. Each boy was invited to participate in a second set of discussion groups with a teacher or teachers of their choice. The only proviso was that either the headteacher or one of her deputy heads was there. An invitation to participate in these discussions was extended to the parents or carers of the boys concerned; in any event the agreement of all parents was secured. It was indicative of the school's commitment to inclusion that the initiative was widely publicised; the discussion group (pupils and teachers) was presented in two school assemblies and a local newspaper made it a news feature. Robin Keith was careful to avoid sensationalism and the charge of patronage: *'I was certainly aware that this was an experiment. I didn't want it to be hijacked for the purposes of selling something we couldn't deliver on. Yet I think it was very important that we showed the lads concerned how we respected the initiative... how we respected them. Two of them, you know, had never been on the school stage in their life'.*

These pupils with problems and their 'chosen' teachers met in a series of timetabled meetings over the course of two terms. The first meeting allowed a set of ground rules for the conduct of the pupil-teacher discussions to be established. The preliminary meeting covered confidentiality. It was agreed that no-one participating in the discussion group should be identified by name in any reporting back to the whole school. It was also agreed that, when accounts were given of classroom events, the real names of teachers and pupils should be disguised. It is noteworthy that both of these suggestions were forthcoming from the pupils, with little prompting from their teachers. It was also agreed that only one person should speak at any one time during the discussions, and that the pupils should have an equal right to state opinions as the teachers. A convention was agreed with regard to language; the use of expletive, whilst not to be admonished in the discussions themselves, was not to be recorded for inclusion in any accounts of the discussions.

The subsequent discussions were on the five areas of concern. As a result the group was able to make the following recommendations:

- 'Wet' lunchtime procedures were to be reviewed
- Teachers were to discuss the idea of a pupil-monitoring form
- Pupils to discuss school rules
- Establishment of a permanent discussion group or School Council
- Headteacher, governor(s) and parent(s) to be invited to attend School Council
- In cases of misbehaviour pupil allowed to 'call a witness'
- Sanctions and Rewards to be kept under review
- Pupil Development Days to be established
- Pupil self-assessment forms to accompany 'report forms'

The final meeting of the group presented these recommendations to the school's senior management team and to a teaching-staff meeting. The recommendations were presented (by one of the pupils and his chosen teacher) to a meeting of the school's Governing Body.

The purpose of the extract is not to show outcomes – in fact, the work at the Cliff School began in autumn, 1997, and is still progressing. It is as yet difficult to assess the progress of the project. What the extract does illustrate, however, is that the process of obtaining the views of all pupils, and particularly those pupils who are regarded as 'problems' should be seen as a positive and non-threatening way of increasing the educational effectiveness of the school for all concerned.

The Cliff School is just one example of a small but increasing number of schools who are including pupils with problems. Linda Ilsam was quick to make the point, on a recent visit I made to the school, that '...*this is as much about process as it is about outcome. All our pupils have benefited from the experience, and the teachers feel happy that they have made the effort. It is not all plain sailing by any means, but we are beginning to see important signs that we may be making progress. Come back to me in three years*'.

Robin Keith was less reserved: '*I said at the outset that the only thing we have to fear from these (pupils with problems) is what others think of us in our dealings with them. The kids are fine... even supposedly hard-liners (disruptive pupils) can be won over. It needs integrity and commitment..and a bit of nerve*'.

Nunc dimittis

Chapter 9

Including the excluded
an agenda

The term 'pupils with problems' is typical of our deference to political correctness. So it is with 'exclusion', which has replaced the more accurate expression 'suspension' at a stroke. Suspension accurately conveys the air of finality that accompanies such actions, as well as the helplessness of the person suspended – given that the rules and processes of appeal are largely outside the cultural domain of the pupil or his family. At the same time, we need to join such children in asking whether what it is that they have been 'suspended' from is supposed to represent a punitive blow by the system: many young people would gladly trade the notoriety of exclusion for the freedom it ultimately gives them.

The origins of the most recent level of official interest in exclusions can be found in the DFE Discussion Paper (DfE, 1992). The document was affected by the work of the National Exclusions Reporting System (NERS), which had been monitoring exclusions from schools over a two year period from the summer of 1990. The findings provided a salutary reminder that the incidence of exclusions was clearly related to certain long-standing factors, many of which also correlate with the characteristics of pupils with problems. Amongst the data originating from this exercise was the confirmation that far more boys than girls were excluded, that 15 was the peak age for exclusion and that there was an over-representation of pupils who had SENs or who were from minority (mainly African-Caribbean) groups.

Since then, exclusions have become a major item on the educational and social agenda, particularly since the new Labour government has given impetus to inclusive practice in its Green Paper. In the same period there has been an avalanche of written material on the subject (see, for example Parsons et al., 1994; Blyth and Milner, 1996; Lloyd-Smith and Davies, 1996). I have indicated that pupils with problems are one of the most problematic groups within the SEN population in schools, in that they are invariably the least likely to secure the sympathy of teachers. Within that group there is a further set of pupils who have rapidly assumed the reputation of untouchables in the education system of England and Wales. These are pupils with problems who are subsequently excluded and for whom the prospect of future education is at best part-time.

This chapter provides a commentary on more recent policy initiatives and the practices that stem from them. It is hoped that the rhetoric of national discussion and collective hand-wringing may be replaced by a lively, local debate which is firmly rooted in the reality of teachers and pupils in schools. Using this alternative strategy may be the most effective way of providing the conditions whereby excluded youngsters can themselves make a conscious decision to participate, rather than being the recipients of unworkable statutory or quasi-autonomous decisions.

I have divided the chapter into three parts. Firstly a scenario is provided for the current debate; this is not an exhaustive summary of what is now an extensive field: this is done elsewhere (see Parsons, 1999; Hayden, 1997). The section explores some of the key themes in the shadowland of exclusionary practice, illustrating the degree to which procedural vagaries still prevail and where pupil and parent advocacy remain conspicuous by their absence. The second part focuses upon the DFE Discussion Paper (*op.cit.*) and on the succeeding Circular 10/94, which map out existing policy arrangements. In this section I will also draw upon some of the burgeoning literature on exclusions, abstracting what appears to be the accepted, though often theoretical, version of what should constitute good practice. These theoretical notions are illustrated by a series of pupil-commentaries, drawn from discussions with groups of excluded Year 11 pupils over the last few months. Using these sections as a conceptual, theoretical and practical base, the third part of the chapter will provide a series of chal lenges to schools and teachers, both as to their ideology and the practical application of proposals that have been made for the inclusion of pupils. Here the over-arching argument suggests that 'quality' in educational provision needs to be measured more by its demo-cratic procedures which secure inclusion for all (or the application of what, in the United States, is termed 'due process') as by the ability of the system to enhance the opportunity of selected groups of children who 'fit' the profile of what is perceived by teachers, parents and others to be 'ideal' learners.

A Scenario for the Current Debate

As already indicated there has been a growing concern about the numbers of pupils being excluded from school since the early 1990s (ACE, 1992b). One connection being made, by politicians and administrators particularly, is the link between problem behaviour in school and a so-called 'juvenile crime wave' which was widely believed to be sweeping the country (again!) during the same period – a point to which I referred earlier. The argu-ments offered in support of this correlation have a familiar ring: that schools, apart from their normative function, are also places where young people can develop social skills which allow them to behave appropriately in the wider context. What is also inferred, however, is that if a young person actually attends school there is a restricted opportunity to engage in anti-social behaviour – or juvenile crime. By excluding pupils, the argument concludes, schools are actually contributing to the crime-wave (sic), a linkage supported by a number of recent studies (Barnardos, 1998).

Notwithstanding this charge, the Education (No. 2) Act (1986) had given schools the right to exclude pupils whose behaviour had, in the school's opinion, become unacceptable. The appeal process, established at the same time, has proved time-consuming, and has often left the pupil in an educational no-man's land. The

Act also reduced significantly the powers and resources of LEA's, yet left them with the responsibility to provide education for excluded pupils. Subsequent to the 1988 Education Act, both grant-maintained and voluntary schools effectively became judge and jury concerning who should be excluded, with little responsibility for the effects of their actions. Finally, Section 22 of the Act identified three types of exclusion: fixed period, indefinite and permanent.

The period from 1986 witnessed an increase in the numbers of pupils excluded from schools, with over 3,000 permanent exclusions reported over a one year period (DFE, 1993). Evidence of this rise in the number of excluded pupils has been supported elsewhere. ACE (1992a) suggested that it was a result of the new procedures incorporated in the Education (No.2) Act: the proportion of calls that this organisation received concerning exclusions rose from 6% in 1988 to 10% the following year. ACE (1992a), summarising one view of this state of affairs, commented that

> Prior to Autumn 1990, permanent exclusion was unheard of, indefinite exclusion rare, and fixed term exclusions tended to be the last disciplinary resort. During the last 18 months, however, fixed term exclusion has become commonplace and indefinite exclusions have increased significantly and are always a prelude to permanent exclusions (p.4).

But whilst there was little doubt that 'the rising number of pupils being excluded from school is causing alarm' (Stirling, 1992), the extent of the problem had proved difficult to ascertain. *The Times Educational Supplement* (1992), for example, reported that even the DFE had expressed misgivings about the validity of the data provided by NERS. Regardless of the uncertainty concerning the actual size of the problem, the DFE Discussion Paper, outlined earlier, signalled its intention to review official policy on the matter and provided the basis for the subsequent legislation in the 1993 Education Act and the policy guidance within the Circular on excluded children (DfE, 1994d). As research by Parsons (1996) and Hayden (*op.cit.*) has bleakly shown, these early estimates may represent the tip of an iceberg.

The 1993 Education Act abolished 'indefinite' exclusions, believing that such an open-ended approach was a licence to abuse. The good intentions of the Act have been subverted by its replacement by 'unofficial' exclusions, which now constitute a significant explanation for a proportion of children being out of school. Instead the Act sanctioned only 'fixed-term' or 'permanent' exclusions. It placed a strict time-scale on the management of permanent exclusions, whilst indicating that a pupil could only be indefinitely excluded on three occasions each term.

In spite of these safeguards, the power of schools to dictate the terms of exclusion have remained largely undiminished. As Hayden (op.cit.) notes, '...the existence of exclusion as a sanction is not called into question', with the headteacher requiring only the backing of the governing body to validate the decision. Only in LEA schools does the Authority have the power to overturn a decision made by the school. In an act of considerable perversity, the 1993 legislation required that LEAs still provided for the educational needs of the pupil once excluded – even though the exclusion might be from a grant-maintained school, and even though LEA support services had been financially emasculated following the 1988 Education Act.

Circular 10/94 provided statutory guidance on how schools and teachers should be responding to excluded pupils. The Circular contained much that was useful and, regrettably, much that was fatuous. In the case of the latter, for example, it stated, as its first guiding principle, that '...parents have a duty to secure the education of their children' (p.3). It was somewhat less forthcoming in placing the same duty on schools to provide, for pupils with problems, the necessary opportunities to exercise this 'duty'. But the Circular did offer some important and positive guidelines for schools, the impact of which has only been weakened by the failure to place a statutory responsibility on them to carry them out. A useful set of 'preliminary factors to consider' was included, together with exemplars of cases when exclusion should not be used. The Circular must be credited with echoing an increasing concern that '...pupils of African/African-Caribbean origin, especially boys, are disproportionately excluded' (p.13).

Since the publication of the Circular more substantial evidence has confirmed what previously had simply been a perception that there had been a rapid rise in the total numbers of children being excluded from school. Parson and Howlett (1996), reporting on a study funded by the DfE, revealed that the rate of increase in exclusions between 1991-1992 and 1992-1993 was 32%, whilst the increase between 1993-1994 and 1994-1995 was 11%. They confirmed that approximately 45% of all exclusions were from Years 10 and 11, and that 'It is likely that over 5,000 15- and 16-year-olds are being permanently excluded and many of them are not returning to mainstream schooling' (*ibid.*, p.110).

'I didn't jump – they shoved me'. The theory and practice of exclusion

Tony's words neatly summarise the debate surrounding the exclusion of certain pupils from schools. It is a complex territory which requires a strong stomach. Recent years have provided evidence that there still remain – in large numbers – schools and teachers who do a fair bit of the shoving.

Firstly, however, a brief overview of how exclusion from school has been theorised. Once again, this is not intended to be a comprehensive review of the literature but a conceptual framework around which the comments of excluded pupils can be arranged. Taken together they provide a powerful rationale for the kind of summary note I received from one parent, that 'Something should be done about this because it's not fair'.

The body of literature on exclusions has grown commensurate with the rise in the numbers being excluded. Hayden (*op.cit.*) provides an extensive review. Acknowledging what have come to be regarded as 'common-sense causes' explaining the phenomenon of exclusion (as opposed to the explanation for an exclusion actually taking place), the literature subsequent to the implementation of the 1988 Education Act has clearly focused upon the effects of the marketing of education, the impact of the National Curriculum, and the demand for accountability. This is unsurprising. Whilst on the one hand promoting a spurious inclusivity through the use of 'charters', the 1988 Act ensured that the concepts of choice and social justice were differentially applicable according to the cultural capital of the individual. In the uneven race towards inclusivity, the pupil with problems is invariably the rank outsider.

The impact of the 1988 Education Act on schools in England and Wales has been described by Bash and Coulby (1989). Ball (1993), in assessing the new climate which pervaded the education system following the Act, says its cumulative effect on teachers provides a new, competitive ethos for their professional operations, in which they '...are now working within a new value context in which image and impression management are more important than the educational process, elements of control have been shifted from the producer (teachers) to the consumer (parents) via open enrolments, parental choice and per capita funding' (p.108). This has created those conditions for special education which critics of the 1988 legislation predicted would materialise. Wedell (1988), for example, engagingly proposed that '...those concerned for the pupils who have SEN are probably justified in expressing doubts as to whether or not the Act will lead to competition between schools in, for example, the adequacy of their support for these pupils' (p.100). Many would now agree that support for pupils with problems, particularly in many mainstream settings, is incapable of sustaining them. Perhaps that is the intention, as Peagam (1991) has pointed out.

In an era in which schools and teachers are under ever-increasing public and political scrutiny, it is likely that many will opt for an exclusionary solution. Thus, as Hayden (*op.cit.*) has remarked, '...the introduction of published league tables of examination results and other indicators of performance in schools has created a climate less likely to be sympathetic to children not only producing no positive contribution to these indicators, but who may also prevent others from doing so' (p.8). This approach has been vigorously promoted in the policy documents of the teacher-unions, demonstrating the extent to which they have moved towards a Rightist agenda.

But the impact of the 1988 legislation was also felt on one of the hidden aspects of exclusion – that of the means-testing of new applicants for primary and secondary school places. Exclusionary conditions now prevail in England and Wales, whereby schools can effectively select their intake. Given the way in which the performance of schools is now measured, most schools will not encourage applications from the parents of children who have a perceived emotional or behavioural difficulty, still less from one who has a pedigree of exclusions from a number of schools within a locality.

Some of these issues are highlighted in the comments of seven boys (Carl, Greg, Nathan, Ray, Troy, Vincent and William) all of whom were excluded in the Spring term of 1998 from schools in the Greater London area. The boys were identified through personal contacts in education and social workers. Each boy was interviewed in his own home. An interview schedule was not followed, the boys being asked to talk about their experiences of exclusion in terms of what led up to the exclusion, the process of exclusion itself and, finally, its aftermath.

Challenging Schools and Teachers

In this section of the chapter eight challenges are made to schools concerning their approach to exclusion; these are based in part on the content of the original Discussion Paper relating to exclusions, on the guidance contained in Circular 10/94, and on the large-scale research evidence which continues to be forthcoming. Some of the individual sections are illustrated by the insights of the seven excluded pupils referred to earlier in this chapter; all, at the time of writing, were recipients of 'home tuition'. Although the challenges were first presented over five years ago (Garner, 1994), little sign of a meaningful response has been forthcoming in the intervening years. They concern both the ideological and practical implications which the debate regarding exclusions appears to raise for schools. School administrators will need to see that 'education for all' becomes a reality rather than remaining merely rhetoric.

Challenge 1: Challenging Schools and Teachers: the relationship between exclusions, social class and culture

Significant recent work on exclusions has linked the phenomenon with domestic deprivation, family disorder and breakdown, and involvement with social services departments (Hayden, *op.cit.*). Such characteristics have long been associated with problem behaviour at school (Furlong, 1985) and identified as indicating the social class of the community from whence such alienated or disruptive pupils are mainly drawn (Tomlinson, 1982). There is now an accepted association between exclusion and pupils with learning difficulties associated with EBD (Galloway et al., 1982); the Special Educational Consortium (1993) went so far as to state that 'An excluded child should, almost by definition, have some sort of emotional and behavioural difficulty or learning difficulty'. So, we are talking about the same population, affected by the same set of disadvantaging conditions.

The problem with such interpretations is that they provide camouflage behind which schools can hide. In much the same way as 'blame' can be allocated exclusively to a pupil, so too can schools utilise environmental factors exclusive to the school to deflect attention from some of the non-inclusionary practices which have pushed the pupil out. Greg makes this point in fairly robust fashion: '*They thought I was mad, needed to see the psychologist. I knew I wasn't so it was like being in a coma and not being able to protest*' and '*That school was rubbish. Total rubbish. I could have told them what it was like, but they didn't listen to me... I was mad, see*'.

There is alternative and currently popular research which suggests that, far from being a neutral backcloth against which pupils engage in a varied series of social and academic interactions, the organisation and ethos of the school itself are crucial determining factors of pupil behaviour (Rutter, et al., 1979; Graham, 1988; Mortimore et al.,1988).

An acceptance by schools that this is the case appears to be of crucial importance if developments are to take place in inter-ser- vice cooperation. The school is at the cutting edge of dealing with educational failure which, in part, is caused by socio-economic disadvantage and by social dislocation. Pupils who are excluded from school need a network of inter-agency support if they are not to fall through the net. One excluded pupil, Ray, was acutely aware of the confusion surrounding his exclusion, commenting that '...*one person didn't seem to know anything about what to do next and it just went on and on. I didn't give a shit after a while because I was leaving soon anyway*'. Refined procedures for communication between educational welfare and social work professionals needs therefore to be given a high priority.

Challenge 2: Publication of statistics concerning exclusions

The Discussion Paper of 1993 suggested that schools should consider publication of their exclusion rates and this has become a statutory requirement. This may have a similar negative effect as does publication of test scores and examination results and the resultant league-tables. The spectre of 'sink schools' remains, if indeed it is not already a reality in some locations. Such institutions, by nature of their inability to attract high pupil numbers, will become under-financed and thus unable to provide a broad, balanced curriculum. There is a strong possibility that teacher-recruitment to such schools will become even more of a problem.

Publication of school-exclusion rates constitutes a bald statement that we have some distance to go before arriving at the inclusive society demanded in the Salamanca Statement (1994) and, more specifically, in the Green Paper. It represents a brutal form of 'naming and shaming', particularly as it is directed towards (frequently) disadvantaged populations.

The advocates of publication believe that the publication of exclusion statistics could act in a positive way: high exclusion rates act as an indicator to parents that a school enforces strict discipline. This interpretation of statistics, however, seems to be as fatuous as the suggestion that parents may view poor performance in SATs as an indication that a school has high academic standards.

If exclusions are to be an essential part of a school's repertoire for dealing with problem behaviour by pupils, the challenge to teachers appears to be at an ideological level. To what extent is conformity to a policy of parental 'need to know' acting against the interests of the development of the whole school, its teachers and certainly against those of the pupil who is excluded? The act of exclusion is clearly detrimental, in short-, medium- and long-term to all three. Schools, if they are unable or unwilling to reduce the level of exclusion, should at least debate the conceptual issues surrounding their actions. The continued failure to recognise the malicious, unproductive and politically-motivated intent behind publication of exclusion rates is little short of staggering.

Challenge 3: Excluded pupils and the National Curriculum

The original Discussion Paper on exclusion refers to the need to ensure continuity of provision under National Curriculum arrangements for those excluded from school. At the same time, there is some suggestion that, in parts, the National Curriculum itself is far too prescriptive, and may itself be a cause of problem behaviour by some pupils. Thus Vincent wanted '...*more stuff which was useful to me, not loads of this and that on things that weren't no concern. They make you stay in school and then just give you rubbish*'. Much of the work attempted with EBD children, particularly in special schools, had been characterised by innovative practice across a range of curriculum areas and pedagogical styles. Much of this work may be inhibited, under the chronic gaze of OFSTED.

Chapter 6 has highlighted some of the background issues and concerns in relation to the continued pre-eminence of the National Curriculum – whatever variants it has, or will in the future, adopt. In this situation, pupils with problems are frequently caught in a curriculum trap. On the one hand many do not receive the direct input they require in respect of the development of a set of social skills designed to self-regulate their responses in problem situations (Carl: '*I know I get mad with people more than I should... and that gets me into trouble... but giving me stuff on France and Spain is not going to help, is it, yeh?'*). On the other they are frequently the recipients of a curricular diet which is at best second-rate, and which because of its irrelevance may compound their feelings of alienation (Vincent: *'I didn't learn a single thing that I can use now. I look back and all I see is that wasted time'*).

Schools have always been under-resourced in their delivery of even the normative curriculum. To establish schemes of work which meet the existing requirements of the National Curriculum and yet capture the imagination and interest of young people requires a considerable commitment of resources. A willingness to plan for these developments may reveal a great deal about the messages that the school gives to those pupils who are at risk of being excluded.

Challenge 4: Establishing and maintaining links with alternative education provision

The original discussion document on exclusions identified weaknesses in the way in which mainstream schools cooperated with off-site units – now PRUs – to which permanently excluded pupils were frequently sent. Traditionally the links between the two had been, at best, tenuous. Whilst Circular 11/94, relating to the education of children other than in mainstream or special schools, called for increased collaboration between schools and PRUs, evidence forthcoming from OFSTED recognised significant problems (OFSTED, 1995). Such difficulties have been uniformly detrimental to those placed in PRUs; Troy exemplified this with his statement that *'Nobody seemed to know what subjects I was doing in GCSEs and a lot of my work got lost'*, whilst Nathan felt bitter that *'Even though I'd done a lot of work and kept out of trouble and my teacher said it would be okay, they (mainstream school) didn't seem prepared to have me back... some teachers even seemed shocked when I showed up'*. A frequent complaint by staff from off-site units is that little consultation takes place between them and the staff of the mainstream school. This lack of communication has often resulted in information concerning the academic profile and the aptitudes of a pupil not being immediately available, so that the unit's ability to make appropriate provision for the pupil is impaired. Carl, for example, felt annoyed that *'Here there's no-one to do DandT and there's no equipment. They won't even have me back in the* (mainstream) *school specially for the class. That's sick, isn't it'*. If not sick it certainly contributes to maintaining the perception, felt by many young people, that they don't really count.

Much closer links are therefore needed between PRUs and mainstream schools. Whilst funding for alternative provision has been severely restricted as a result of financial restraints imposed by successive governments, there is much useful work which could be done to develope or refine liaison arrangements and promote staff and curriculum development. For too long have PRUs and their 'off-site unit' antecedents been regarded as the poor relation in this education partnership. From a pragmatic standpoint alone, it is in the interests of schools to plan for the future, given that at least some of the pupils who have been excluded may well be reintegrated.

Challenge 5: Ownership of problems relating to excluded pupils

This challenge takes us to the heart of the debate concerning inclusive practice and its application across the full range of SENs. The present system of exclusions makes it very easy for some schools to abrogate their responsibilities to those who behave inappropriately by excluding them. Schools have assumed substantial powers in this respect, following the 1986 Act. Hand in hand with this is a belief that 'attitudes in the school(s) have hardened towards children with emotional and/or behavioural difficulties' and that there 'has been a very sharp shift away from supportive strategies towards punitive measures' (ACE, 1992a). Nathan's view on this was that *'...I knew pretty soon after I went to that school that I wouldn't last long. They made a lot of promises, were okay for a couple of weeks and then they started...*

always picking on me'. A similar situation was encountered by William, who said that '*...as soon as I got in trouble they were after getting rid of me... Pownall* (deputy headteacher) *even said so*'.

The NERS data indicated that exclusion numbers are highest in the 15 year-old age group, a view confirmed by subsequent research (Imich, 1994; Parsons *et al.*, *op.cit.*). This represents a critical stage of adolescent and educational development, during which time educational and vocational orientations are reinforced. It also marks a point at which a substantial number of the 15,000 hours (sic) of schooling have elapsed. It would seem, in this age of charters, contracts and learning guarantees, that it ought to be incumbent on schools to make a positive declaration of commitment to all its pupils before this stage is reached. Greg expressed a mild sense of shock at '*...being left with nothing... and after I had done some good things, and could have got a few (GCSE) passes*', whilst Troy believed that '*...the school wanted me out quickly and didn't give a shit about what was down for me from then on*'.

If we are functioning, as politician, pundit and management guru have it, in an age of accountability, it is surely the case that the time has come for schools to be required to indicate a formal commitment to educate all pupils to compulsory leaving age once they have reached, say, 14 years. Although there may be legal (and practical) pitfalls in implementing this it seems logical that if schools have subscribed to the laws of the market – then these should be applied equally for the benefit of producer *and* consumer (as they purport to do in the commercial sector).

Challenge 6: Incorporating the views of pupils with problems, and those of their parents

As indicated elsewhere there has been little evidence that the views of pupils with problems concerning their schooling have been used to develop or refine school procedures or professional practice. Nor has their voice played a significant role in negotiation or arbitration at the point of exclusion. A shared approach to strategies needs to be encouraged by schools. This may be a useful preventative measure too, whereby the incorporation of the views of disruptive pupils may mean that they are 'brought back in' to normative processes of the school, rather than being 'pushed out' (De Ridder, 1989) by them.

With hindsight Robin believed that he '...*could have been alright if they'd listened. I didn't want to get kicked out... all my mates were there... but it didn't matter what I said. They didn't even listen to my Mum*'. Vincent echoes this feeling of helplessness: '*I wanted to go back for a while in the first few weeks* (following exclusion) *but then I thought there'd be no point. Nothing is going to change. Foster* (headteacher) *is always right...*'

In a similar vein, input from parents of pupils who are excluded, or who are at risk of being so, needs to be encouraged. ACE (1992a) noted serious concern about the procedures that are followed in this respect. Parents have been critical of the ways in which schools have liaised with them, feeling in many cases that they had not been sufficiently consulted before things came to a head. Moreover, ACE (1992a) reported that a number of families had been denied their legal rights during the exclusion process, with schools simply failing to follow the correct legal procedures. Dialogue between home and school needs to be refined in such a way that the procedures are not alienating for the families of the excluded young person: '*My folks said that they were glad I was out, because they were treated like shit... made to feel it's their fault... made to feel small. My Dad was the angriest...*' (Troy).

Challenge 7: Schools should be discouraged from excluding pupils

Recent governments, and the present administration have pursued education policies which rest on a punitive market-orientated ideology, where 'successful' schools are rewarded for being able to attract more pupils and hence more money. Many schools have entered enthusiastically into this race to attract pupils (providing, of course, such pupils are of the 'right sort). The reverse should apply when schools lose pupils through exclusion. This ought particularly to be the case in Years 10 and 11, which are crucial in the academic life of the pupil; they also represent that time of a pupil's school career when one would expect that an 'efficient' school had established a workable pattern of discipline and a supportive ethos for even the most problematic of cases. In other words, the level of exclusion in a given school should be an indicator of whether or not that school is, in contemporary hyperbole, failing.

Schools should be discouraged from excluding pupils by a series of financial disincentives. Whilst it must be acknowledged that a small percentage of pupils will behave so badly and over so long that even schools which have proven records of low exclusion will be forced to exclude, it remains the case that other schools are relatively unsuccessful in dealing with such pupils. Subject to certain safeguards it appears efficacious not only that funding should follow the pupil, but also there should be some form of 'claw-back' applied, so that, in a sense, the school makes a financial reimbursement for the job it has failed to do. Once again there are some obvious difficulties – but the power of the cash register may have to be used as positive sanction to secure inclusion.

Challenge 8: Schools who successfully retain pupils should be encouraged

Schools which have a track-record of working successfully with pupils with problems, and who consequently have low exclusion rates, should be financially rewarded. The true financial cost of exclusion has been the focus of some recent attention (Barnardos, *op.cit.*). There is a well-established link between exclusion and delinquency, and the likelihood that the pupils involved will become career criminals (Devlin, 1996). The net cost to society is immense. Whilst it is true to say that by no means all of the roots of such criminal careers are nurtured in schools, there is a straightforward logic in suggesting that the cycle of offending may best be broken by enhancing education at an early age. This needs to be done especially in respect of pupils with problems – a recommendation which itself is probably as old as the incidence of problem behaviour in schools.

As schools are 'rewarded' for academic excellence by OFSTED approval and by the occasional plaudit from the Chief Inspector, so too should they accrue real benefits if they succeed in retaining pupils who may be prone to exclusion. In spite of arguments to the contrary, little official attention is given to the social and economic conditions of a school's pupil-roll in assessing that school's merits. One possibility is that a national schools award, along the lines of the Schools' Curriculum Award, could be considered. This would represent a public recognition of the school's success in social education. Just as some schools have begun to be recognised for their policy of inclusion, and for their ability to provide for those who have special educational needs, schools who succeed with pupils at risk of exclusion should be celebrated and publicised.

Amidst so many other burning issues in education in the 1990s the question of how schools deal with those pupils with problems who are at risk of exclusion should be viewed as one hallmark of 'quality'. For this to happen the schools themselves need to respond to some of the challenges outlined here.

EPILOGUE

'Telling lies to the young is wrong. Proving to them that lies are true is wrong' (Yevgeny Yevtushenko)

Educational provision for pupils with problems, always a contentious and ideologically polarised matter, is now more than ever in the news. Taking as an exemplar the *Times Educational Supplement* (July 10, 1998), it is possible to gauge the scale and extent of the concern currently being expressed, in political, professional and public domains. Many of the items highlighted as newsworthy reflect issues at the heart of this book, ranging from a plea to take a fresh look at a 'Strategy to boost disaffected youth', via commentaries on the new 'literacy straitjacket' and a likely return to 'tried and tested' methods of teaching maths, to the observations that 'Half of children in care skip school', that those in care are more likely to be excluded from them and that financial instability is hampering the youth service. To this negative cocktail may be added, almost as an aside, the headline from the same issue: 'More failing schools to close'.

It is doubtful if Hieronymous Bosch could have painted a more brutal, self-serving and soulless utopia. Following the election of the first Labour administration for 20 years in May, 1997, there was hope for thoughtful, person-centred government. Here was an opportunity, in health, welfare and education particularly, to reformulate some of the major policy initiatives of Thatcherite Britain. How bitter, then, the realisation that not much has changed. For Tory, read New Labour. In consequence this is still a land in which the young by their thousands have been duped into dead-end training; where pupils in schools see the chances of educational experiences which meet their needs disappear as curriculum constraints are reinforced; where schools continue as blunt instruments by which the descendants of the New Right can ensure conformity; where thousands of teachers with ideals, ideas and commitment are designated as incompetent on the whim of a Chief Inspector whose own capability in the classroom, all those years ago, excaped scrutiny and where pupils with problems remain as educational and social outcasts in a system which had exchanged interest in principles and people for pound notes and profit: Education plc.

The expression 'rational fears', to which this book alludes, more sensibly describes the overall scenario facing pupils who engage in behaviours which are seen as problematic. What is apparent is that the concerns, widely voiced in England and Wales at present, are a further expression of the traditional fear of difference – whether cultural, racial, social or behavioural – within our society. The fear is not for the safety, well-being and future prospects of the current batch of 'pupils with problems'.

Nor do there appear to be many innovative rabbits in the hat of central government. Kenny sums up the failed attempts of a generation to make a difference: *'They look at me as if I'm stupid. Like they've always looked at me. You can't do this or you can't do that lot that I was sick of before I got out of primary school... and if I have to give you a reason why I'm here* (Secure Unit) *I'd say that it is because of all of those people like you who make a living out of me. We're the pit-ponies of today, we are'.*

Fortunately there remain many – both pupils and teachers – who believe that there still might be a change for the better. It is those teachers and learners operating in micro-systems, who offer cause for optimism. In the absence of any forthright commitment to a coherent, resourced and, above all, nationwide programme for pupils with problems, the best prospects appear to lie at grassroots level, in the hearts and minds of those who daily struggle to define and meet real educational and social needs of such pupils; and in ensuring that localised autonomy and inclusion processes, involving young people as active agents, remain intact.

Bibliography

Adams, R. (1991) *Protests by Pupils*. Lewes: Falmer Press

Ainscow, M. (1997) Teacher Education, Special Needs and Inclusive Schooling. Some Lessons from Around the World, in J. Davies and P. Garner (eds.) *At the Crossroads. Special Educational Needs and Teacher Education*. London: David Fulton

Armstrong, D. and Galloway, D. (1994) Special educational needs and problem behaviour: making policy in the classroom, in S. Riddell and S. Brown (eds.) *Special Educational Needs Policy in the 1990s*. London: Routledge

Armstrong, D., Galloway, D. and Tomlinson, S. (1993) Assessing Special Educational Needs: the child's contribution, *British Educational Research Journal*, 19, 121-131

Ashworth, W. (1954) *The Genesis of Modern British Town Planning*. London: Routledge

Atkinson, P., Delamont, S. and Hammersley, M. (1988) Qualitative research traditions: a British response to Jacob. *Review of Educational Research*, 58 (2), 231-250

Ayers, H., Clarke, D. and Murray, A. (1995) *Perspectives on Behaviour*. London: David Fulton

Ball, S. (1993) Education markets, choice and social class. *British Journal of the Sociology of Education*. 14 (1), 3-20.

Barton, L. and Oliver, M. (1992) Special Needs: Personal Trouble or Public Issue?, in Arnot, M. and Barton, L. (eds.) *Voicing Concerns*. Wallingford: Triangle Press

Barton, L. and Tomlinson, S. (eds.) (1984) *Special Education and Social Interests*. Beckenham; Croom Helm

Bash, L. and Coulby, D. (1989) *The Education Reform Act: competition and control*. London: Cassell

Bash, L., Coulby, D. and Jones, C. (1985) *Urban Schooling: theory and practice*. Eastbourne: Holt, Rinehart and Winston

Basini, A. (1981) Urban schools and 'disruptive' pupils, *Educational Review*, 33 (3), 37-49

Blandford, S. (1998) *Managing Discipline in Schools*. London: Routledge

Blyth, E. and Milner, J. (1996) *Exclusion from School*. London: Routledge

Bond, L. and Compas, B. (Eds.) (1989) *Primary Prevention and Promotion in the Schools*. Newbury Park, CA: Sage

Booth, C. (1896) *Life and Labour of the People in London*. London: Macmillan

Booth, T. and Coulby, D. (eds.) (1987) *Producing and Reducing Disaffection*. Milton Keynes: The Open University Press

Bovair, K. (1993) A Role for the Special School, in J. Visser and G. Upton (eds.) *Special Education in Britain after Warnock*. London: David Fulton

Bronfenbrenner, U. (1979) *The Ecology of Human Development*. Cambridge: Harvard University Press

Buist, M. (1980) Truants talking. *Scottish Educational Review*, 12 (1), 40-51

Burland, R. (1979) Behaviour Modification in a Residential Special School for Junior Maladjusted Boys: A Review. *Journal of the Association of Workers for Maladjusted Children*. 7 (2)

Bush, L. and Hill, T. (1993) The right to teach, the right to learn. *British Journal of Special Education*, 20 (1), 4-7

Byrne, D., Williamson, B. and Fletcher, B. (1975) *The Poverty of Education*. London: Martin Robertson

Cabot, R. (1931) Treatment in social casework and the need for tests of its success and failure. *Proceedings of the National Conference of Social Work*, London

Canter, L. (1982) *Assertive Discipline*. San Francisco: Jossey-Bass

Capel, S., Leask, M. and Turner, T. (1995) *Learning to Teach in the Secondary School*. London: Routledge

Carson, J. (1938) The Relationship of Mental Defect to Juvenile Delinquency. *The Special Schools Quarterly*. XXVI (2), June, 36-44

Charlton, T. (1996) Where is control located?, in K. Jones and T. Charlton (eds.) *Overcoming learning and Behaviour Difficulties*. London: Routledge

Children's Legal Centre (1988) *Evidence to the Department of Education and Science Committee of Enquiry into Discipline in Schools*. London: CLC

Children's Society (1993) *Passing the Buck.Institutional Responses to Controlling Children with Difficult Behaviour*. London: The Children's Society

Clark, C., Dyson, A., Millward, A. and Skidmore, D. (1995) *Innovatory Practice in Mainstream Schools for Special Educational Needs*. London: HMSO

Cole, T. and Visser, J. (1998) How Should the 'Effectiveness' of Schools for Pupils with EBD be Assessed? *Emotional and Behavioural Difficulties*, 3 (1), 37-43

Cole, T., Visser, J. and Upton, G. (1998) *Effective Schooling for Pupils with Emotional and Behavioural Difficulties*. London: David Fulton

Cooper, P. and McIntyre, D. (1996) *Effective Teaching and Learning*. Buckingham: Open University Press

Cooper, P. (1989) Respite, relationships and re-signification: a study of the effects of residential schooling on pupils with emotional and behavioural difficulties, with particular reference to the pupils' perspective. Unpublished PhD thesis. School of Education, University of Birmingham

Cooper, P. (1993) *Effective Schools for Disaffected Students*. London: Routledge

Cooper, P. (1996) Giving it a Name: the value of descriptive categories in educational approaches to emotional and behavioural difficulties. *Support for Learning*, 11 (4), 146-150

Cooper, P., Smith, C. and Upton, G. (1990) Training for Special Educational Needs: the qualifications and training requirements of teachers in schools for pupils with emotional and behavioural difficulties in England and Wales. *British Journal of In-Service Education*. 16 (3), 188-195

Cooper, P., Smith, C. and Upton, G. (1994) *Emotional and Behavioural Difficulties*. London: Routledge

Coulby, D. (1984) The creation of the disruptive pupil, in Lloyd-Smith, M. (ed.) *Disrupted Schooling*. London: John Murray, 98-119

Coulby, D. and Coulby, J. (1995) Pupil Participation in the Social and Educational Processes of a Primary School, in P. Garner and S. Sandow (eds.) *Advocacy, Self-advocacy and Special Needs*. London: David Fulton

Coulby, J. and Coulby, D. (1989) Intervening in Junior Classrooms, in J. Docking (ed.) *Education and Alienation in the Junior School*. London: Falmer

Courtman, D. (1996) The Role of Emotion in Pastoral Care and Personal and Social Development: The Emotional Curriculum, *Pastoral Care in Education*, 14, (4), 3-6

Cox, C. and Boyson, R. (1977) *The Black Papers*. London: Temple Smith

Croll, P. and Moses, D. (1985) *One in Five*. London: Routledge and Kegan Paul

Crozier, J. and Anstiss, J. (1996) Out of the Spotlight: Girls' Experience of Disruption, in M. Lloyd-Smith and J. Davies (eds.) *On the Margins. The Educational Experience of 'Problem' Pupils*. Stoke on Trent: Trentham Books

Cullingford, C. (1991) *The Inner World of the School*. London: Cassell

Dale, R. (1979) The Politicisation of School Deviance: Reactions to William Tyndale, in L. Barton and R. Meighan (eds.) *Schools, Pupils and Deviance*. Driffield: Nafferton Books

Dalin, P. (1978) *The Limits to Educational Change*. London: Macmillan

Daniels, H. (1990) The Modified Curriculum: Help with the Same or Something Completely Different?, in P. Evans and V. Varma (eds.) *Special Education: Past, Present and Future*. Lewes: Falmer Press.

Darling, J. (1994) *Child-Centred Education and its critics*. London: Paul Chapman Publishing

Davie, R. and Galloway, D. (eds.) (1995) *Listening to Children in Education*. London: David Fulton Publishers

Davies, J. and Garner, P. (1997) *At the Crossroads. Teacher Education and Special Educational Needs*. London: David Fulton

Dawson, R. (1984) Disturbed pupils' perception of their teachers' support and strictness. *Maladjustment and Therapeutic Education*, 1 (3), 24-7

Dempster, L (1989) Dangerous units remain open, *The Times Educational Supplement*, 3 February

Department for Education (1992) *The Initial Training of Secondary School Teachers: New Criteria for Courses* (Circular 9/93). London: DfE

Department for Education (1993) *Exclusions. A discussion paper.* London: DfE

Department for Education (1993) *The Initial Training of Primary School Teachers: New Criteria for Courses* (Circular 14/93). London: DfE

Department for Education (1994) *The Organisation of Special Educational Provision Circular 9/94,* London: DfE

Department for Education (1994a) *Pupil Behaviour and Discipline. Circular 8/94.* London: DfE

Department for Education (1994b) *The Education of Children with Emotional and Behavioural Difficulties.* Circular 9/94. London: DfE

Department for Education (1994c) *Exclusions from School.* Circulars 10/94. London: DfE

Department for Education (1994d) *The Education by LEAs of Children Otherwise than at School.* Circulars 11/94. London: DfE

Department for Education (1994e) *Code of Practice on the Identification and Assessment of Special Educational Needs.* London: DfE

Department for Education and Employment (1997) *Requirements for Courses of Initial Teacher Training Circular 8/94.* London: DfEE

Department for Education and Employment (1997a) *Excellence for All Children. Meeting Special Educational Needs.* London: DfEE

Department for Education and Employment (1997b) *Draft Guidance on LEA Behaviour Support Plans.* London: DfEE

Department of Education and Science (1978) *Special Educational Needs* (The Warnock Report). London: HMSO

Department of Education and Science (1985a) *A Survey of Provision for Pupils with Emotional/Behavioural Difficulties in Maintained Special Schools and Units.* London: DES

Department of Education and Science (1985b) *Better Schools.* London: DES

Department of Education and Science (1988) *The Education Reform Act.* London: DES

Department of Education and Science (1989) *Inquiry into Discipline in Schools* (The Elton Report), London: HMSO

Department of Health (1989) *The Children Act.* London: HMSO

Devlin, A. (1995) *Criminal Classes.* Winchester: Waterside Press

Docking, J. (1989) Elton's four questions: some general considerations, in N. Jones (ed.) *School Management and Pupil Behaviour.* Lewes: Falmer

Drakeford, B. (1997) *The Whole-School Audit.* London: David Fulton

Drew, D. (1990) From tutorial unit to schools' support service. *Support for Learning,* 5 (1), 13-21

Edgecumbe, R. (1977) *The Boundary between Education and Therapy.* London: FAETT

Elliott-Kemp, J. (1986) *SIGMA a Process-based Approach to Staff Development,* Sheffield City Polytechnic: Pavic Publications

Emler, N. and Reicher, S. (1995) *Adolescence and Delinquency.* Oxford: Blackwell

Engels, F. (1969) *The Condition of the Working Class in England*. London: Granada (first published in 1892)

Everhart, R. (1983) *Reading, Writing and Resistance*. Boston: Routledge and Kegan Paul

Farrell, P. (1996) *Children with Emotional and Behavioural Difficulties*. London: Falmer Press

Fisher, D. (1996) *Pupil Referral Units*. Slough: NFER

Fletcher, J. (1847) Moral and educational statistics of England and Wales, *Journal of the Statistical Society*, 10, 193-233

Fletcher, J. (1847) Moral and educational statistics of England and Wales, *Journal of the Statistical Society*, 11, 344-66

Fletcher, J. (1847) Moral and educational statistics of England and Wales, *Journal of the Statistical Society*, 12, 151-335

Fletcher, J. (1847) *Summary of the Moral and educational statistics of England and Wales*. London: private publisher

Fletcher, S. (1996) Mentoring and the Form tutor. Paper to the British Educational Research Association Conference, Lancaster University

Fletcher, P. and Presland, J. (1990) Contracting to overcome adjustment problems. *Support for Learning*. 5 (3), 153-158

Fletcher-Campbell, F. (1996) *Resourcing of Special Educational Needs*. Slough: NFER

Ford, J., Mongon, D. and Whelan, M. (1982) *Special Education and Social Control*. London: Routledge and Kegan Paul

Fordham, D. (1989) Flexibility in the National Curriculum, *British Journal of Special Education*, 16, 50-52

Freeman, M. (1987) Taking children's rights seriously, *Children and Society*,1, 299-319

Fulcher, G. (1989) *Disabling Policies*. Lewes: The Falmer Press

Fullan, M. (1982) *The Meaning of Educational Change*. New York: Teachers College Press

Furlong, V. (1985) *The Deviant Pupil*. Milton Keynes: Open University Press

Furtwengler, W. (1990) Improving school discipline through involvement, in C. Moles (ed.) *Student Discipline Strategies*. Albany, NY: State University of New York Press

Gains, C. and Garner, P. (1996) Models of Intervention for Children with Emotional or Behavioural Difficulties. *Support for Learning*, 11 (4), 141-145

Galloway, D., Ball, T., Blomfield, D. and Seyd, R. (1982) *Schools and Disruptive Pupils*. London: Longman.

Garner, P. (1987) Disruptive Pupils: a study of two approaches in a London Borough. Unpublished MA Thesis. University of London: Institute of Education

Garner, P. (1992) Involving 'disruptive' students in school discipline structures. *Pastoral Care in Education*, 10 (3), 13-19

Garner, P. (1993) A Comparative Study of the Views of Disruptive Students in England and the United States. Unpublished PhD dissertation. University of London: Institute of Education

Garner, P. (1994) Advocacy and the young person with special educational needs. *International Journal of Adolescence and Youth.* 5 (1), 47-60.

Garner, P. (1996) Schools by Scoundrels: the views of 'Disruptive' Pupils in Mainstream Schools in England and the United States, in M. Lloyd-Smith and J. Davies (eds.) *On the Margins. The Educational Experience of 'Problem' Pupils.* Stoke on Trent: Trentham Books

Garner, P. (1996) 'A la recherche du temps PRU: case study evidence from off-site and pupil referral units'. *Children and Society,* 10 (3), 187-196

Garner, P. (1996) A Special Education? The experiences of Newly Qualifying Teachers during training. *British Educational Research Journal,* 20 (2), 155-163

Garner, P. and Sandow, S. (1993) Can education prevent crime?, *Pastoral Care in Education,* 11, (4), 25-29

Garner, P. and Sandow, S. (eds.) (1995) *Advocacy, Self-Advocacy and Special Needs.* London: David Fulton

Gersch, I., Holgate, A. and Sigston, A. (1993) Valuing the child's perspective: a revised student report and other practical initiatives. *Educational Psychology in Practice,* 9 (1), 35-45

Gillborn, D., Nixon, J. and Ruddock, J. (1993) *Dimensions of Discipline. Re-thinking Practice in Secondary Schools.* London: HMSO

Goffman, E. (1959) *The Presentation of Self in Everyday Life.* New York: Doubleday

Gribble, D. (1993) *Stand up, stand up! Stand up for your rights.* London: Ed. Lib

Gross, J. (1996) Implementing Individual Behaviour Plans. *Special Children*

Gurney, P. (1990) The Enhancement of Self-esteem in Junior Classrooms, in J. Docking (ed.) *Education and Alienation in the Junior School.* Basingstoke: The Falmer Press

Hall, J. (1997) *Social Devaluation and Special Education.* London: Jessica Kingsley Publishers

Halliday, J. (1996) *Back to Good Teaching.* London: Cassell

Hanko, G. (1985) *Special Educational Needs in Ordinary Classrooms.* London: Basil Blackwell

Hargreaves, D. (1967) *Social Relationships in a Secondary School.* London: Routledge and Kegan Paul

Hargreaves, D. (1982) *The Challenge for the Comprehensive School.* London: Routledge and Kegan Paul

Hargreaves, D., Hester, S. and Mellor, F. (1975) *Deviance in Classrooms.* London: Routledge and Kegan Paul

Harris, K. (1982) *Teachers and Classes. A Marxist Analysis.* London: Routledge and Kegan Paul

Hayden, C. (1997) *Children Excluded From Primary School*. Buckingham; Open University Press

Herbert, M. (1981) *Behavioural Treatment of Problem Children*. London: Academic Press

Her Majesty's Chief Inspector (1995) *Pupil Referral Units. The first twelve inspections*. London: OFSTED

Her Majesty's Inspectorate (1987) Education Observed 5. *Good Behaviour and Discipline in Schools*. London: HMSO

Hewton, E. (1988) *School Focused Staff Development*. Lewes: Falmer

Heyman, R. (1979) Comparative education from an ethnomethodological perspective. *Comparative Education*, 15 (3), 241-249

Hobbs, N. (1975) *The Futures of Children*. San Francisco: Jossey-Bass

Hoghughi, M. (1983) *The Delinquent. Directions for Social Control*. London: Burnett Books

Home Office (1995) *Young People and Crime. Home Office Research Study 145*. London: Home Office Research and Statistics Department

Humphries, S. (1981) *Hooligans or Rebels? An Oral History of Working Class Childhood and Youth 1889-1939*. Oxford: Blackwell

Hutton, W. (1995) *The State We're In*. London: Jonathan Cape

Inner London Education Authority (1985) The Relationship Between Emotional Disturbance and Learning Difficulties. Report of the 1985 ILEA Day EBD Schools Conference. Unpublished

Jones, K. and Charlton, T. (eds.) (1996) *Overcoming Learning and Behaviour Difficulties*. London: Routledge

Kanner, J. (1962) Emotionally Disturbed Children: A Historical Review, *Child Development*, 33, 97-102

Kauffman, J. (1985) Educating Children with Behaviour Disorders, *Special Education*, 249

Khaleel, M. (1993) *Pupil Councils First Independent Monitoring Programme*. Liverpool: PAD

Kinder, K., Wakefield, A. and Wilkin, A. (1996) *Talking Back: Pupil Views on Disaffection*. Slough: NFER

Kinder, K. and Wilkin, A. (1996) Disaffection: What are effective school-based strategies? Paper to the British Educational Research Association Conference, Lancaster University

Konig, K. (1959) *The Human Soul*. Edinburgh, Floris Books

Kounin, J., Friesen, W. and Norton, E. (1966) Managing emotionally disturbed children in regular classrooms, *Journal of Educational Psychology*, 57, 1-13

Kumar, V. (1993) *Poverty and Inequality in the UK. The effects on children*. London: National Children's Bureau

Lacey, C. (1970) *Hightown Grammar*. Manchester: Manchester University Press.

Lang, P. (1990) Responding to Disaffection: Talking About Pastoral Care in the Primary School, in J. Docking (ed.) *Education and Alienation in the Junior School*. Basingstoke: The Falmer Press

Laslett, R. (1990) Could do Better, *Maladjustment and Therapeutic Education*, 8 (2), 107-111

Lawrence, J., Steed, D. and Young, P. (1989) *Disruptive Children – Disruptive Schools?* London: Routledge and Kegan Paul

Lebas, E. (1981) *City, Class and Capital*. London: Edward Arnold

Levine, R. and Campbell, D. (1979) *Ethnocentrism*. New York: Wiley

Lewis, A. (1996) Summative National Curriculum assessments of primary aged children with special needs. *British Journal of Special Education*, 23 (1), 9-14

Lewis, R. (1977) Artful dodgers of the world unite in C. Cox, and R. Boyson, *Black Paper 1977*. London: Temple Smith

Lloyd-Smith, M. (ed.) (1984) *Disrupted Schooling*. London: John Murray

Lloyd-Smith, M. and Davies, J. (1996) *On the Margins. The Educational Experience of 'Problem' Pupils*. Stoke on Trent: Trentham Books

Lovey, J., Docking, J. and Evans, R. (1993) *Exclusion from School*. London, David Fulton

Lowenstein, L. (1975) *Violent and Disruptive Behaviour in Schools*. Hemel Hempstead: NAS/UWT

Lunt, I., Evans, J., Norwich, B. and Wedell, K. (1994) Collaborating to meet special educational needs: Effective clusters? *Support for Learning*, 9 (2), 73-78

Malik, M. (1993) *Passing the Buck. Institutional responses to controlling children with difficult behaviour*. London: The Children's Society

Marchant, S. (1995) The Essential Curriculum for Pupils Exhibiting Emotional and Behavioural Difficulties. *Therapeutic Care and Education*, 4, (2), 36-47

Marsland, D. (1995) *Towards Teacher Professionalism*. York: CRE

Maxim, P. (1989) An Ecological Analysis of Crime in Early Victorian England. *The Howard Journal of Criminal Justice*, 28 (1), 37-50

Mayhew, H. (1861) *London Labour and the London Poor*. London

McCall, L. and Farrell, P. (1993) Methods used by educational psychologists to assess children with emotional and behavioural difficulty, *Educational Psychology in Practice*, 9 (3), 164-170

McDonnell, L., McLaughlin, M., Morison, P. (eds.) (1997) *Educating One and All: students with disabilities and standards-based reform*. Washington: National Academy Press

McManus, M. (1989) *Troublesome Behaviour in Class*. London: Routledge

McNamara, D. (1992) The Reform of Teacher Education in England and Wales; teacher competence; panacea or rhetoric?, *Journal of Education for Teaching*, 18, (3)

McNamara, E. (1987) Behavioural contracting with secondary aged pupils. *Educational Psychology in Practice*. 2 (4), 21-6

Meijer, C., Pijl, S. and Hegarty, S. (eds.) (1994) *New Perspectives in Special Education*. London: Routledge

Mongon, D. and Hart, S. (1989) *Improving Classroom Behaviour: New Directions for Teachers and Pupils*. London: Cassell

Morris, E. (1998) Speech to the Seventh British Appraisal Conference, Stockport, 26 January

Mortimore, J. and Blackstone, T. (1982) *Disadvantage and Education*. London: Heinemann

Mortimore, P., Davies, J., Varlaam, A. and West, A. (1984) *Behaviour Problems in Schools: An Evaluation of Support Centres*. Beckenham: Croom Helm

Mortimore, P., Sammons, L., Stoll, L. and Ecob, R. (1988) *School Matters*. London: Open Books

Murray, C. (1990) *The Emerging Underclass*. London: Institute of Economic Affairs

Murtaugh, M. and Zeitlin, A. (1989) How serious is the motivation problem in secondary education? *High School Journal*, 72, February/March

Musgrove, F. (1964) *Youth and Social Order*. London: Routledge and Kegan Paul

National Curriculum Council (NCC) (1989) *A Curriculum for All*. York: NCC

Nelken, D. (1989) Discipline and Punish: Some Notes from the Margin. *The Howard Journal of Criminal Justice*, 28 (4), 245-254

Normington, J. and Boorman, B. (1996) Development, procedures and good practice at Westfields Education Provision, Kirklees, *Support for Learning*, 11 (4), 170-172

O'Brien, T. (1997) Challenging Behaviour: challenging an intervention. *Support for Learning*, 12 (1) 162-164

O'Brien, T. (1998) *Promoting Positive Behaviour*. London: David Fulton

O'Hagan, F. and Edmunds, G. (1982) Pupils' attitudes towards teachers' strategies for controlling disruptive behaviour. *British Journal of Educational Psychology*, 52, 331-40

O'Hear, A. (1988) *Who Teaches the Teachers?* London: Social Affairs Unit

Office for Standards In Education (1993) *Achieving Good Behaviour in Schools*. London: HMSO

Office of Standards in Education (OFSTED) (1993) *School Inspection Handbook*, London: HMSO

Office for Standards in Education (1995a) *Guidance on the Inspection of Nursery and Primary Schools*. London: HMSO

Office for Standards in Education (1995b) *Guidance on the Inspection of Secondary Schools*. London: HMSO

Office for Standards in Education (1996a) *Pupil Referral Units. The first twelve inspections*. London, HMSO

Office for Standards in Education (1996b) *Guidance on the Inspection of Primary Schools*. London: HMSO

Palmer, C., Redfern, R., and Smith, K. (1994) 'The Four P's of Policy'. *British Journal of Special Education*, 21, (1) 4-6

Parsons, C. and Howlett, K. (1996) Permanent exclusions from school: A case where society is failing its children. *Support for Learning*, 11 (3), 109-112

Parsons, C. (1999) *Excluded Children*. London: Routledge

Peagam, E. (1995) The Foolish Man Built His House Upon The Sand: A response to DfE Circular 2 – The Education of Children with Emotional and Behavioural Difficulties. *Therapeutic Education and Care*, 4 (1), 9-16

Pearson, G. (1983) *Hooligan. A History of Respectable Fears*. London: Macmillan

Phillips, M. (1996) Back to school – To be de-Educated. *The Observer*, Sunday, 8 September, 14-15

Plaskow, M. (1985) Class of '85, in R. Rogers (ed.) *Education and Social Class*. Lewes: Falmer Press

Potts, W. (1917) The Moral Defective. *The Special Schools Quarterly*, VII (1 and 2), 5-38

Pyke, N., Prestage, M. and Dean, C. Police fear growing tide of exclusions. *Times Education Supplement*, 19 November

Raymond, J. (1987) An Educational Psychologist's Intervention with a Class of Disruptive Pupils using Pupil Perceptions, *Educational Psychology in Practice*, 3, 16-22

Reid, K., Hopkins, D. and Holly, P. (1986) *Towards the Effective School*. Oxford: Blackwell

Reynolds, D. (1976) The Delinquent School, in P. Woods (Ed.) *The Process of Schooling*. London: Routledge and Kegan Paul

Reynolds, D. (1985) *Studying School Effectiveness*. Lewes: Falmer Press

Reynolds, D. (1989) Effective Schools and Pupil Behaviour, in N. Jones (ed.) *School Management and Pupil Behaviour*. Lewes: Falmer Press

Richman, N. and Lansdown, R. (eds.) (1985) *Problems of Pre-school Children*. Chichester: John Wiley

Rimmer, A. (1990) Death of a School. *Therapeutic Care and Education*, 1 (1), 53-59

Rimmer, A. (1994) *Personal Communication*

Rist, R. (1970) Student social class and teacher expectations: the self-fulfilling prophecy in ghetto education. *Harvard Educational Review*, 40, 411-451

Robertson, J. (1989) *Effective Classroom Control*. London: Hodder and Stoughton

Roffey, S. and O'Reirdan, T. (1997) *Infant Classroom Behaviour*. London: David Fulton Publishing

Rogers, C. (1961) *On Becoming a Person*. Boston: Houghton Mifflin Co

Rogers, W. (1992) Students who want the last word, *Support for Learning*, 7, (4), 166-170

Rosenthal, R. and Jacobsen, L. (1968) *Pygmalion in the Classroom*. New York: Holt, Rinehart and Winston

Royer, E. (1995) Behaviour Disorders, Exclusions and Social Skills: Punishment is not Education. *Therapeutic Care and Education*, 4 (3), Winter, 32-36

Rutter, M. and Madge, N. (1976) *Cycles of Disadvantage*. London: Heinemann

Rutter, M., Maughan, B., Mortimore, P. and Ouston, J. (1979) *Fifteen Thousand Hours: Secondary Schools and their Effects on Pupils.* London: Open Books

Sacken, D. (1989) School Disciplinary Processes, *Urban Education,* 23

Sanders, D. and Hendry, L. (1997) *New Perspectives on Disaffection.* London: Cassell

Saunders, M. (1979) *Class Control and Behaviour Problems.* London: McGraw-Hill

Scarlett, P. (1989) Discipline: pupil and teacher perceptions. *Maladjustment and Therapeutic Education,* 7 (3), 169-77

School Curriculum and Assessment Authority (1996) *Supporting Pupils with Special Educational Needs.* London: SCAA

Schools Councils U.K. (1994) *Growing up with Pupil Councils.* Liverpool: Schools Councils U.K

Schostak, J. (1983) *Maladjusted Schooling.* Lewes: Falmer Press

Sebba, J. with Sachdev, D. (1997) *What Works in Inclusive Education.* London: Barnardos

Sewell, T. (1997) *Black Masculinities and Schooling: how Black boys survive modern schooling.* Stoke on Trent: Trentham books

Sheldon, B. (1994) Social Work Effectiveness Research: Implications for Probation and Juvenile Justice Services. *Howard Journal of Criminal Justice,* 33 (3), 218-235

Sheppard, B. (1988) *Off Site Pupils and their Experience of Schooling.* London: Institute of Education, Post-16 Centre

Siegel, M. (1982) *Fairness in Children.* London: Academic Press

Smith, C. (1988) There's nothing more practical than a good theory. *Maladjustment and Therapeutic Education.* 6 (3), 146-147

Smith, C. (1990) The management of children with emotional and behavioural difficulties in ordinary and special schools, in V. Varma (ed.) *The Management of Children with Emotional and Behavioural Difficulties.* London: Routledge

Smith, C. (1996) Special needs and pastoral care: bridging a gap that shouldn't be there. *Support for Learning,* 11 (4), 151-156

Special Educational Needs Training Consortium (1996) *Professional Development to Meet Special Educational Needs.* Stafford: SENTC

Spindler, G. (1955) *Education and Anthropology.* Stanford University Press: Stanford

Stallworth, W., Frechtling, J. and Frankel, S. (1983) In-school suspension: A Pilot Program. *ERS Spectrum,* 1 (1), 23-31

Steiner, R. (1910) *Anthroposophie, Pyschosophie, Pneumatosophie.* Dornach: GA 115

Stenhouse, L. (1979) Case study in comparative education: particularity and generalisation. *Comparative Education,* 15 (1), 5-10

Stevenson, D. (1991) Deviant Students as a Collective Resource in Classroom structures, *Pastoral Care in Education,* 10, 13-19

Thomas, G. (1992) Write on or Write-off? *British Journal of Special Education.* 21 (1) 12

Thomas, G., Walker, D. and Webb, J. (1998) *The Making of the Inclusive School.* London: Routledge

Tomlinson, S. (1982) *A Sociology of Special Education.* London: Routledge and Kegan Paul

Tonnies, F. (1955) *Community and Association.* London: Routledge and Kegan Paul

Townsend, P. (1979) *Poverty in the United Kingdom.* Harmondsworth: Penguin

Turkington, R. (1986) In Search of the Disruptive Pupil: Problem Behaviour in Secondary Schools 1959-1982. Unpublished PhD thesis. Department of Sociology, University of Leeds

Stuart, R. (1971) Behavioural Contracting within the Families of Delinquents. *Journal of Behaviour Therapy and Experimental Psychiatry*, 2, 1-11

UNESCO (1994) *The Salamanca Statement and Framework for Action on Special Needs Education.* Paris: UNESCO

Upton, G. (1983) *Educating Children with Behaviour Problems.* Cardiff: Faculty of Education, Cardiff University

Varma, V.(ed.) (1993) *Management of Behaviour in Schools.* London: Longman

Wade, B. and Moore, M. (1993) *Experiencing Special Education.* Buckingham: Open University Press

Walker, D. (1977) William Tyndale in C. Cox, and R. Boyson, *Black Paper 1977.* London: Temple Smith

Weber, K. (1982) *The Teacher is the Key.* Milton Keynes: Open University Press

Wedell, K. (1988) The new Act: a special need for vigilance. *British Journal of Special Education*, 15 (3), 98-101

Westmacott, E. and Cameron, R. (1981) *Behaviour Can Change.* Basingstoke: Globe Education

Williams, A. (1996) Curriculum auditing: an accessible tool or an awesome task. *British Journal of Special Education*, 23 (2), 65-69

Willis, P. (1977) *Learning to Labour.* Farnborough: Saxon House

Wirth, L. (1938) Urbanism as a way of life. *American Journal of Sociology*, 44, 3-24

Woods, P. (1979) *The Divided School.* London: Routledge and Kegan Paul

Woods, P. (1990) *The Happiest Days?* Basingstoke: Falmer Press

Index